isement Contractors, 30, Southampton Street, Strand, W.C.

## GEORGE E. BISHOP,
### Professional Tutor & Agent,

Prepares Ladies and Gentlemen for Theatres or Music Halls, and procures Engagements. Easy payments (or part Salary), and Stamped Agre⸺ to every Pupil.

*A bona-fide Training School and Agency.*

### 1, CATHERINE STREET, STRAND, W.C.

| | |
|---|---|
| **10** | ### MISS MARIE LLOYD<br>The Oxford Favourite.<br><br>In her New Song " 'ARRIET'S REPLY," an answer to Alber Chevalier's " Coster's Serenade." Specially produced. |
| **11** | ### THE FLETCHERS<br>The Accomplished Skaters. |
| **12** | ### MISS HARRIET VERNON<br>The Po⸺ |
| **13** | ### BESSIE BONEHILL, ⸺personator. |
| **14** | ### Æ⸺ |
| **15** | ### ELSA ⸺EL<br>The Charming Bravura ⸺pra |
| **16** | ### DAN LENO, The Inimitable⸺ |
| **17** | ### ROSE SULLIVAN<br>The Irish Brilliant. |
| **18** | ### HENDERSON & STANLEY QUARTETTE<br>Vocalists and Instrumentalists. |
| **19** | ### SISTERS REEVE<br>Duettists and Dancers. |

Conductor of the Orchestra ... ... ... Mr. E. BOSANQUET.

**Open at 7.30, Commence at 8 o'clock.**

**Grand Morning Performance every Saturday at 3.**

**Sole Manager, Mr. C. R. BRIGHTEN**

The order of this Programme is liable to alteration, and on Saturdays the Management reserves the right to alter it in its entirety.

Hart Street, Covent Garden.

# MARIE LLOYD

## Queen of the Music-halls

## MISS MARIE LLOYD.

Is received with great enthusiasm upon her return to the Oxford.

# MARIE LLOYD

## Queen of the
## Music-halls

### Richard Anthony Baker

ROBERT HALE · LONDON

ISBN 0 7090 4135 7

Robert Hale Limited
Clerkenwell House
Clerkenwell Green
London EC1R 0HT

Photoset in Goudy Old Style by
Derek Doyle & Associates, Mold, Clwyd.
Printed in Great Britain by
St Edmundsbury Press Limited
Bury St Edmunds, Suffolk.
Bound by WBC Bookbinders Ltd, Bridgend, Glamorgan

# CONTENTS

# ILLUSTRATIONS

### Photographs

### Line Illustrations

PICTURE CREDITS

Tony Barker: 1, 4, 6, 9–10, 13. Roy Waters: 2–3, 5, 7, 11–12, 15. *The Entr'acte*: 17–23.

# ACKNOWLEDGEMENTS

The author wishes to thank Barrie Anthony, Les Ball, Tony Barker, Alan Owen, Michael Pointon, Tomme Thomas, Roy Waters and John Whitehorn for their help, as well as copyright holders for their permission to reprint extracts from the following copyright material:

*Book of the Musical Theatre*, Kurt Ganzl and Andrew Lamb (Bodley Head)

*Carriages at Eleven*, W. MacQueen-Pope (Rupert Crew)

*The Diary of Virginia Woolf*, Anne Olivier Bell (The executors of the estate of Virginia Woolf and the Hogarth Press)

'Every Little Movement Has a Meaning of Its Own'; 'Folkestone for the Day'; 'I Can't Forget the Days when I was Young'; 'A Little of What You Fancy Does You Good'; 'Piccadilly Trot'. (EMI Music Publishing).

*Florence Desmond*, Florence Desmond (Harrap)

*I Had Almost Forgotten*, C.B. Cochran (Harbottle and Lewis)

*Immoment Toys*, James Agate (The executors of the estate of James Agate and Jonathan Cape)

'A Little of What You Fancy Does You Good'; 'Piccadilly Trot' (Redwood Music)

*Music in London*, George Bernard Shaw and a letter by Shaw, published by the *Pall Mall Gazette* on 16 October 1894 (The executors of the estate of Bernard Shaw and the Society of Authors)

*My Autobiography*, Charles Chaplin (Bodley Head)

*My Early Life*, Winston Churchill (Octopus)

*Selected Essays*, T.S. Eliot (Faber and Faber)

*Some of These Days*, Sophie Tucker (Barrie and Jenkins)

*Take it for a Fact*, Ada Reeve (William Heinemann)

*Winston S. Churchill*, Randolph S. Churchill (William Heinemann)

# Chapter 1

## 1870–85

# THE BIRTH OF MARIE LLOYD

It began in 1885 in the Eagle music-hall, just off London's City Road. Marie, a petite, fair-haired girl with slightly protruding teeth, was taken there by her father, who worked there as a barman in the evenings. One night, Marie, decked out in a polonaise dress with a mantilla of black lace over her head, sang two songs. The first was 'In the Good Old Times', written by one of the small band of successful music-hall songwriters, Fred Gilbert:

> When I was a girl and a nice girl I was,
> At least so the young men asserted.
> Society was far better than now
> If now it's correctly reported.
> The ladies of fashion felt no sudden passion
> To flash their good looks on the stage.
> No Lily or Langtry would climb up the slang tree
> In hope to become all the rage.
> In the good old times long ago (long ago),
> In the good old times long ago
> In the good old times
> There were no such crimes
> As our daily paper shows.

Marie, still known then by her real name – Matilda Alice Victoria Wood – was just fifteen when she flashed her good looks on the stage. She owed this appearance to her father's job as a barman at the Eagle. Known to his friends as Brush, John Wood was one of many working in the Hoxton area of Shoreditch as an artificial flower-maker supplementing his weekly wage of £2 5s by working as a barman in the evenings. Brush Wood had no theatrical ability; but, on the other side of the family – Marie's mother, also Matilda – there *was* talent. Matilda's sister was on the boards as a dancer, working under the exotic name of Madame Louise Patti; and Alice Archer, the daughter of her brother, became well known in her day as a comedienne, Lily Lena.

John Wood and Marie's mother, Matilda Archer, moved to Hoxton from Bethnal Green, where they married in April 1869. Nine-and-a-half months later – on 12 February 1870 – Matilda was born. The family nicknamed her Tilly. She was followed by a boy, also John, then Alice, and then seven other children, two of whom died young.

Hoxton, where Marie was born, was a poor area. Some people living near her home in Plumber Street (now Provost Street) were struggling well below the poverty line. Hoxton, though, was nowhere near as bad as nearby Wapping, which, according to Charles Booth, the compiler of a mammoth late Victorian survey of London, appeared 'to stagnate with a squalor peculiar to itself'. (Booth 1902/3) Charles Booth took a liberal view of the East End music-halls: 'The keynote is a coarse, rough fun and nothing is so much applauded as good step dancing. Of questionable innuendo, there is little, far less than at West End music halls.' (Booth 1902/3)

Of Hoxton in general, Sir Walter Besant wrote: 'Its people [are] quiet and industrious, folk who ask for nothing but steady work and fair wages. Everybody quite poor; yet, the place has a cheerful look. There may be misery, but it is not apparent. The people in the streets seem well fed and are as rosy as London smoke and fog will allow.'

Both Marie and Alice attended Bath Street School, a short distance from their home. Inspectors consistently praised the school's musical ability. In 1880, one wrote: 'The singing and articulation would be noteworthy anywhere. In such a neighbourhood as this, they are exceptionally so.' (School Board for London, Inspector's report, Finsbury Division, Bath Street School).

After leaving school, Marie tried a number of jobs. She made babies' boots; she curled feathers; but she soon put in her notice. The return of Madame Patti from a trip to the Continent seems to have set her sights seriously on entertaining.

Her first opportunity to follow in her aunt's footsteps came through her local parish church, St John the Baptist. To help raise funds for the Band of Hope, Marie staged a show featuring a troupe she coyly titled the Fairy Bell Minstrels. Alice's contribution was the recital of a doleful poem, called 'The Dead Doll'. It began:

You needn't be trying to comfort me.
I tell you my dolly is dead.

She died of a broken heart,
And a dreadful crack on the head.

Many years later, Alice credited Marie with the work of director:

> I recited these lines according to Marie's minute instructions. A
> dramatic gesture towards the direction of the deceased doll; my hand
> over my heart to indicate the broken heart; and a thump on my own
> head to demonstrate the whack that killed the doll. (*Lloyds Sunday
> News* 1922)

In an interview, Marie recalled that a song she sang had a dramatic
effect on at least one member of the audience: 'A man in the audience
… had brought a bottle of whisky … but, when I sang a beautiful ditty
with the soul-stirring title of Throw Down the Bottle and Never Drink
Again, he quickly and unostentatiously hurled the bottle at his
luckless wife and, in stentorian tones, declared that he would never
touch intoxicating liquors again.' (*The Strand* February 1912)

It seems odd to view Marie as a youthful preacher of temperance,
given that alcohol eventually played a part in ruining her life. The
Fairy Bell Minstrels, though, enjoyed success in a minor way. After St
John the Baptist, Marie and Alice, decked out in little velvet dresses
with puff sleeves, performed at a charity bazaar at the Congregation-
alists' City Temple at Holborn Viaduct. Afterwards, the Temple's
founder, Dr Joseph Parker, called the girls over and balanced them on
his knees. 'Who taught you to recite?' he asked Marie. 'No one,' she
replied. 'I taught myself.' 'And who taught you, little girl?' he asked
Alice. 'She did,' said Alice, pointing at Marie.' (*Lloyds Sunday News*)

By now, Marie was set on music-hall as a career. She could hardly
avoid it. It was in her family;[1] and music-halls were all around her.
Within a 2-mile area around her home, there were no fewer than 150
halls, most of them just parts of pubs, but some larger ones, too – like
the Eagle.

The Grecian theatre and the Eagle music-hall, which stood just
round the corner from her home, were popular meeting-places, where
people could dance, drink and be entertained. A contemporary
advertisement gives some idea of what was on offer: 'Concerts in the
open air, dancing and vaudeville in the saloon, set paintings,
cosmoramas, fountains, grottoes, elegant buildings, arcades, colon-
nades, grounds, statuary, singing, music to render in a fairy scene, of
which a due estimation can only be formed by inspection.' (A
contemporary handbill)

Charles Dickens gave a rather breathless description of the gardens
in which the Grecian and the Eagle stood in *Sketches By Boz*.

There were the walks, beautifully gravelled and planted – and the refreshment boxes, painted and ornamented like so many snuff-boxes – and the variegated lamps shedding their rich light upon the company's heads – and the place for dancing ready chalked for the company's feet – and a Moorish band playing at one end of the gardens and an opposition military band playing away at the other. (Dickens, 1836/7)

For many years, the most spectacular pantomimes in London were to be seen at the Grecian, produced by George Conquest, a theatre manager, a writer of melodrama, a clever maker of props, an acrobat and a reasonable actor, too, despite a stutter. He was also a first-rate talent scout, helping to find fame for two comedians who were to rule the London pantomime scene in later years. One was a big, jolly comic called Herbert Campbell who enjoyed great success at his first London pantomime at the Grecian in 1875. And Conquest's *Jack and the Beanstalk*, produced at the Surrey Theatre in 1886, featured the other, a young Dan Leno, making his first appearance in a London pantomime.

Music-hall had already spawned some talented entertainers. They were the old guard: Alfred Vance and George Leybourne, who vied with each other over the blueness of their songs; G.H. MacDermott, whose greatest success, 'By Jingo', dating from the Russian-Turkish wars, introduced the word 'jingoism' into the language; Jenny Hill, known as the Vital Spark, and Bessie Bellwood, whose imprecations silenced hecklers at a stroke: ('If you open your mouth any more, you'll spit up your past life'). None of these early stars lived beyond the age of 50.

By the time Marie made her début at the Eagle, early in 1885, George Conquest had relinquished his interest. In that time, the theatre had been reopened for only a few months. During its closure, it had been under the control of William Booth of all people, the founder of the Salvation Army, then a relatively new religious movement. He looked upon the Grecian as a sink of iniquity, in which 'lost souls' and 'wicked sinners' danced their way to perdition. He bought the lease with the intention of gathering together 'tens of thousands of the lowest classes [to rejoice] in the Lord'. While trying to raise the £16,750 needed, he turned to the Archbishop of Canterbury, Archibald Campbell Tait. With a £5 donation, Tait became the first prominent Anglican to support the Salvation Army. He took the same view of the Grecian; but the theatre's leading actor, John Clynds, saw it rather differently: he said players were 'no more distasteful to public decency nor injurious to public morals than some of the exhibitions of the Salvation Army'.

Clynds defence of the theatre earned him the public thanks of the

Church and Stage Guild, which had been formed only three years previously with the aim of breaking down prejudice against the stage by the Church. The Salvation Army eventually became embarrassed about owning licensed premises and pulled out.

George Conquest had done his best to make the Grecian the sort of place to which a man might take his teenage daughter. He published rules in his programmes:

> No boys or young girls admitted into the new hall or permitted to dance on the platform.
>
> No person of known immorality admitted into the grounds, theatre or hall.
>
> Any person committing any breach of decorum or making use of offensive or improper language will be immediately expelled.

Most proprietors did their best to ensure their music-halls were respectable. But they had many opponents, who were convinced things were as bad as they had been 20 to 30 years previously. During the 1870s, licences were withheld from at least three halls against which complaints of drunkenness and immorality had been frequently made: the Alexandra Theatre and Highbury Barn at Islington, the Cremorne Gardens in Chelsea and the Argyll Rooms near Piccadilly Circus. The 1860s had seen the closure of two smoky and rowdy supper rooms – the sort of meeting-places in which music-hall was born. They were the Coal Hole in the Strand and the Cyder Cellars in Covent Garden, where unashamedly pornographic songs were sung – songs with titles like 'The Bower That Stands in Thigh Lane' and 'He'll No More Grind Again'. By Marie's times, these male-only Caves of Harmony had disappeared. Their place was taken by purpose-built music-halls – theatres of style and comfort, in which men and women were welcome. Compared with the songs of early music-hall, Marie's choruses were virtual hymns, even though they still landed her in trouble.

In 1885, music-hall was about to enter its most productive and spectacular era. The old guard was disappearing. Larger and larger audiences were being attracted to the growing number of smart halls. The new theatres were, by and large, the sort of place a man could take his wife to. A new generation of singers and comedians was urgently needed. The demand was met. Two men, who were to dominate music-hall's Golden Age, were waiting in the wings. Little Tich made his London début just a few weeks before the start of 1885; and Dan Leno made his first London appearance as comedian and clog dancer in October that year.

Marie Lloyd, too, was waiting. Just a week after she sang 'In The Good Old Times' at the Eagle in 1885, she was earning five shillings a turn at three other halls. She was still Matilda Wood then. She briefly changed her name to Bella Delmeyer, at times rendered Delmere, Delmare, and in other ways, too.

She also experienced her first brush with the law. In addition to 'In The Good Old Times', she was regularly singing a wistful little song, 'The Boy I Love is up in the Gallery':

> The boy I love is up in the gallery.
> The boy I love is looking now at me.
> There he is. Can't you see?
> Waving his handkerchief,
> As merry as a robin that sings on a tree.

Unfortunately, a singer called Jessie Acton owned the rights to 'In The Good Old Times', and another entertainer, Nelly Power, owned 'The Boy I Love'. Marie soon smoothed their ruffled feathers, and found other songs to sing.

Within a short time, she had a piece of luck. Appearing at the Falstaff in Old Street, another music-hall near her home, she was spotted by a well-known agent, George Belmont. She sang only one song, but she was encored four times. Belmont signed her up, but she immediately broke the contract by appearing at another music-hall. Belmont was furious and threatened to sue her. But, with the same charm she had used on Jessie Acton and Nelly Power, she calmed him down. Even so, she soon had a new manager, George Ware, an agent known in the business as the Old Reliable, and the composer, curiously enough, of 'The Boy I Love'. Ware wrote two songs especially for Marie – 'He's All Behind' and 'You Should Go To France'. Ware loved her act, but hated her name: Bella Delmeyer had to go. 'No one could get on with a name like that. Change it. Now, wherever you go, what name do you see? Lloyd. Lloyds on the railway bridges, Lloyds on the walls, Lloyds on the Sunday newspaper.' (*Lloyds Sunday News* 1922) So, Marie Lloyd was born.

# Chapter 2

## 1885

# THE ANTI-MUSIC-HALL CAMPAIGNERS

As Marie began to take the first steps of her career, the killjoys, who regularly pestered her, began to organize themselves. One of the most active anti-music-hall campaigners was Frederick Charrington, who renounced a £1 million fortune from his family – Charrington, the brewers – in favour of promoting temperance. At that time, music-hall proprietors had to apply annually to the courts for licences. Charrington opposed their applications for two reasons: he did not like the heavy drinking that went on, and he did not like the prostitutes who frequented some halls. Charrington took stern measures against them when he learned that even people harbouring prostitutes were breaking the law, irrespective of whether the women were soliciting. His leaflets painted a lurid picture:

This Way To The Pit of Hell

You can go to the theatre or music-hall and there your eyes can gaze upon the indecent dance and there you can hear the filthy song, but, unless you are born again, you can never see the glories of Heaven and you will never hear the song of the redeemed. (Thorne 1913)

Charrington handed out many of these tracts outside Lusby's music-hall.[2] Not surprisingly, its owners, George Adney Payne and Charles Crowder, were not amused. In February they brought a High Court action against Charrington. In the course of the evidence, Charrington portrayed Lusby's as as wicked a place as the Cremorne Gardens and the Coal Hole had been a generation earlier. During four-and-a-half hours in the witness box, he expanded on his theory that 'the [music]-hall is the way to hell'. At the end of the case an order was granted restraining him; but he continued harassing Lusby's clientele – this time with a pamphlet entitled 'Battle of the Music Halls'. A few weeks later, Crowder returned to court to try to get him imprisoned. But the judge merely ordered Charrington not to continue circulating the leaflet, unless it had offensive references to Lusby's removed.

Then, in July, General Booth's wife, Catherine, and the social reformer Josephine Butler persuaded William Stead, the muck-raking editor of a magazine called *Pall Mall Gazette*, to publish a series of articles on child prostitution. Their aim was to help to push through Parliament the Criminal Law Amendment Bill, which, in part, increased the age of consent from thirteen to sixteen. The articles, titillating in style, were a sell-out. In a wide-ranging review of all that contributed to loose morals, the articles, entitled 'Maiden Tribute to Modern Babylon', found wickedness in the theatre. 'It is said that, at a certain notorious theatre, no girl ever kept her virtue more than three months ... Some theatrical managers are rightly or wrongly accused of insisting upon a claim to ruin actresses whom they allow to appear on their boards.

The Salvation Army, capitalizing on the public mood, launched a so-called national purity campaign. Four thousand people signed a petition supporting the bill. Thousands more attended a rally in Hyde Park, and a number of public meetings were held throughout July and August. At one, it was resolved to form a National Vigilance Association 'for the enforcement and improvement of the laws for the repression of criminal vice and public immorality'. (*The Sentinel 1885*) Its chairman was the Liberal MP George Russell. On the committee, were, among others, the Bishop of London, Frederick Temple; Frederick Charrington; William Stead and the Booths' son, William Bramwell.

Stead and Booth were somewhat overzealous in their efforts to prove that, as the law stood, it was easy to buy a young girl for prostitution or slavery. They arranged to acquire a girl themselves, albeit with the knowledge of her mother. The stunt backfired on them and they appeared at the Old Bailey charged with abduction. Booth was acquitted, but Stead was sent to prison for three months.

The activities of the National Vigilance Association were publicized in its official magazine, *Vigilance Record*, edited by another tireless anti-music-hall campaigner, Laura Ormiston Chant, a composer of hymns who devoted part of her life to helping to run a lunatic asylum. She acknowledged that many people saw her as 'an imperious, sour-visaged, unhappy, wretched, miserable Puritan, who wanted to make London unspeakably dull'. (*Camberwell and Peckham Times* 3 November 1894) Undeterred by being caricatured by *Punch* as

Prowlina Pry, Mrs Ormiston Chant explained her views about music-hall at a meeting of the Playgoers' Club:

> The music-hall supplies a class of entertainment to suit people, who, out of sheer tiredness of brain or want of a superior education, could hardly appreciate a play ... The music-hall caters for people, who have a small proportion of brains ... They have not reserve power enough to cater for themelves and therefore someone else must do it for them. (*Chant* 1895)

Although the Bishop of London closely associated himself with the National Vigilance Association, not all his clergymen supported its violent opposition to music-hall. The way the Church treated the Reverend Stewart Headlam showed what could happen when clergymen stepped out of line. Headlam was curate at St Matthew's, Bethnal Green, the church where Marie's parents were married. But he fell foul of the ecclesiastical hierarchy when he gave a lecture about theatre:

> [I used to think] music-halls very low places – merely from popular opinion, for I had hardly ever been to one; but I am bound to say that they seem to me now, with one or two great faults, to meet a want which we don't find met by a theatre. They are cheaper, they are more free-and-easy, you can go for a shorter time and yet see a complete entertainment for that short time and they encourage a different kind of art. (*Era* October 1877)

Headlam told his audience that a mainstay of the music-hall was the solo singer, and he criticized silly and coarse songs:

> I believe that really good songs would be as popular as silly ones. 'Let me write the songs. I don't care who writes the sermons', said someone; and there is no doubt that Mr MacDermott or George Leybourne have far more influence in London than the Bishop of the diocese ... I have not said anything about what to many is the main evil of music-halls – that, in some cases, they are much frequented by loose women. I don't think it at all fair to blame a place for the people who go there. I also think that the large proportion of music-hall audiences are respectable working people and clerks. But that prostitutes do go there is undeniable. But I don't think that is any reason why respectable people should keep away – rather, perhaps, all the more reason why they should go; if some of the wives and sisters of the upper and middle classes would go and not let their brothers and husbands say music-halls are not fit places for them, it would indeed be well. (*Era*, October 1877)

It was this last statement which caused the scandal. Frederick Temple's predecessor, Bishop John Jackson, wrote to Headlam: 'I do pray earnestly that you may not have to meet before the Judgment

Seat those whom your encouragement first led to places where they lost the blush of shame and took the first downward step towards vice and misery.' (Bettany 1926)

As a result of the lecture, Headlam was stripped of his curacy. He took up other work, including the post of Secretary of the Church and Stage Guild. After Bishop Jackson's death in January 1885, Headlam tried to win the approval of Frederick Temple. A meeting was arranged in October 1885 between Temple and a small delegation representing the Guild, including Headlam and the actor Ben Greet. Their discussion centred on the ballet. Bishop Temple underlined his views on the subject in a letter to Headlam: 'I am confident that, to the vast majority of young men and young women, the sight of such dancing, as now practised, is a very grievous temptation. To encourage them to go into temptation, when Our Lord has taught them to pray that they may not be led into temptation, is, in my opinion, most mischievous.' (Bettany 1926)

Headlam was later to become a fan of Marie: 'Such people as Marie Lloyd ... have been genuine artists ... Marie Lloyd ... may be audacious sometimes, but an artist – surely. If art is criticism of life, you get first-hand criticism there.' (*The Sunday Times* 1916). But this was in years to come. In 1885, Marie had hardly cut her professional teeth.

# Chapter 3
## 1885–89
# MARRIAGE, MOTHERHOOD AND THE CRITICS

It is not clear exactly when Marie appeared for the first time at the Eagle. But the *Era*, the main theatrical newspaper of the day, carried this advertisement on 20 June 1885:

Royal Eagle Music Hall, City Road
On Monday evening and every evening during the week, the following artists will appear:
George Bellvere, Marie Lloyd, George Vokes, Carrie Wilson, Brothers Morton, Fred Hamilton, Nellie Clare, Fred Carlos, Miss Annie d'Lonra.

There was no review of the performance and there was no mention of Marie working at any other hall. In September, though, she earned a couple of lines of praise. The *Era* carried an advertisement for the Royal, Holborn (later rebuilt and renamed the Holborn Empire). At the top of the bill was Patrick Feeney, who called himself the Irish ambassador; somewhere in the middle was Harry Randall, just beginning to make a name for himself as a comedian, and at the bottom was Marie, who styled herself a serio-comique. In October, the *Era* commented: 'Marie Lloyd ... kept it briskly going'. Another paper, the *Entr'acte*, was more prescient: 'Marie Lloyd ... must be regarded as a youthful vocalist of promise.'

Later that month, she was at another famous hall – Collins on Islington Green. Randall appeared there, too, as did Herbert Campbell and Katie Lawrence, a few years before the latter caused a storm with 'Daisy Bell' (Daisy, Daisy, Give Me Your Answer Do). Then, in November, she appeared at yet another well-known hall – the Metropolitan in Edgware Road. It was inevitable that Marie would work alongside many entertainers on their way up; and so it was at the

Met. Here she appeared with the comedian Charles Coborn, just a few months before he bought 'Two Lovely Black Eyes'.

That Christmas, Marie was at Collins. Among the growing band of young male admirers in the audience was a music-hall devotee, George Foster, who was to become one of the most accomplished agents in the business.

> [Marie] was dressed as a girl sailor with blue satin blouse, short white skirt and white socks and, on her head, she was wearing a straw hat, cocked at the pertest of angles. Her face was as pretty as a picture. Her laughing mouth showed an upper row of pearly, if slightly protruding teeth. Her flashing eyes were full of defiance and devilment.
>
> She 'got' the house instantly. She was down to sing one number only. It was this:
>
> My Harry's a sailor
> On board of a whaler
> I love my Harry
> And Harry loves me.
> When he comes home from sea
> 'Tis married we will be.
>
> When Marie got to the second verse, she completely forgot her lines. She stopped dead, laughed at her own discomfiture, leaned over the floats and whispered to the conductor. She then broke into a rollicking hornpipe. Could Marie Lloyd dance? I'll say she could.
>
> At the end, she ran off the stage to a positive ovation. If ever an artist made an instantaneous hit, it was Marie Lloyd.
>
> It was not because Marie was especially brilliant ... She ... triumphed by sheer personality and charm. (Foster 1939)

George Foster made a point of getting to know Marie, as did many other young men. Another suitor was Gus Leach, the son of the manager of the Varieties Theatre, Hoxton, known locally as 'the flea-pit'. But Foster fell in love with Marie and they became engaged. He made one big mistake, though. In the bar of the Cambridge music-hall he introduced her to one of his best friends, Percy Courtenay, whom he described as 'a young blood and racing man with plenty of money and an attractive personality'. (Foster 1939) When Marie ended her relationship with Foster and became engaged to Courtenay, it became the talk of the music-hall world. It even provided the idea for a coster song. – 'Never Introduce Your Donah (*Girlfriend*) to a Pal',[3] written by A.E. Durandeau and sung by another comedian on his way up, Gus Elen.

In January 1886, Marie was back at Collins on a bill that included the red-nosed comic James Fawn, who was to become famous as the singer of 'If You Want to Know the Time, Ask a Policeman'. At Collins, Marie again attracted the attention of the *Entr'acte* critic: 'Marie Lloyd ... gives serio-comic songs in a very acceptable fashion.'

At this stage she must have worked more dancing into the act, for, in February, when she celebrated her sixteenth birthday, she dropped the description 'serio-comic' and began calling herself 'the terpsichorean serio'. At the South London Palace in Lambeth she appeared on a bill with Bessie Bellwood and G.H. MacDermott. The *Entr'acte* declared: 'Marie Lloyd ... evidently takes as a model, Miss Lottie Collins' (the dancer who was the first to throw herself into the energetic 'Ta-Ra-Ra-Boom-De-Ay').

By Easter 1886, word had spread throughout the music-hall world that Marie was rather better than the average new turn. She appeared then at one of the West End's most prestigious halls, the Oxford, near the junction of Oxford Street and Tottenham Court Road. Many years later, a writer in the *Encore* described the impact she made on this first appearance in the West End.

> She came on with every sign of complete self-possession and confidence in her own ability, but it was a quiet confidence, not aggressive. She sang a very ordinary serio-comic song 'That's where the young man smiles' and then 'Oh Jeremiah'. Neither of the songs was worthy of her rendering, but she got all there was out of them. Then, she came on in a white muslin dress and gave a pastoral song 'I wonder, oh I wonder where you are', finishing with a skirt dance. This was a very dainty effort and it roused the audience to a pitch of enthusiasm that was only possible in the old days. She was recalled again and again.

(The lyrics of 'Oh Jeremiah' were as follows:

> My Jerry was an errand boy to Wilson, Webb and White
> He used to work from five a.m. till half past six at night
> He said he never would be rich wheeling loaves of bread
> So he told me he'd go to sea and this is what I said.
>
> Oh Jeremiah, don't you go to sea
> Oh Jeremiah, stay at home with me
> Your ship may go to pieces down, down below
> You'd all be drowned and never be found, blown to Jericho.)

During Marie's first week at the Oxford, she became the talk of West End theatre people, and by the Saturday matinee the theatre was crowded with pros. The *Encore*'s writer was there too:

Some of the remarks I heard were very scathing. 'She can't dance.' 'It's all fake.' 'What can they see in her?' And 'She won't do for the provinces' were a few of the criticisms. Then, a very good friend of mine, Lieutenant Albini, the distinguished conjuror, who had a clever daughter of his own, spoke up. He said 'Now, look here. You've said some nasty things about that little girl, but, in my opinion, she's all talent and mark my words, she'll go a long way in the profession. She'll reach a higher position than anyone in this hall today.'

In September Marie was at the Middlesex in Drury Lane (later the Winter Garden): 'Marie Lloyd is an enterprising and genial singer and dancer and her various essays, which are everywhere well appreciated and applauded, are in great favour at the Middlesex' (Entr'acte 25 September 1886), and in October she was at the Paragon with both Dan Leno and Little Tich: 'Marie Lloyd in dance and song continues her successful career'. (Entr'acte 30 October 1886)

The plaudits continued during 1887. In January she was at the Royal Foresters in Bethnal Green: 'Marie Lloyd ... has always characterised her efforts with every symptom of success' (Entr'acte 29 January 1887); in May she was at the Canterbury on the same bill as Jenny Hill and the great male impersonator, Vesta Tilley: 'Marie Lloyd sang and danced her way into everybody's favour' (Era 14 May 1887); in June she returned to the Metropolitan: 'Marie Lloyd is highly successful and deservedly so' (Entr'acte 11 June 1887), and in August she was back at the Oxford: 'Marie Lloyd ... is deservedly one of the cleverest step dancers on the stage. She was enthusiastically applauded.' (Era 6 August 1887) After that came a brief provincial tour, playing, among other places, Birmingham, Hull and Chatham.

In the meantime, her romance with Percy Courtenay proceeded apace. He was a good talker and, best of all, he made Marie laugh. She agreed they should marry – a decision one of her music-hall friends, Flo Hastings, thought foolish: 'He was a dirty old thing. One night at the Standard, he came up to me and used filthy language just as I was going on. I flung a drink in his face and the barman nearly killed him.' (Farson 1972)

The wedding was held on 12 November at St John the Baptist church, where Marie had formed the Fairy Bell Minstrels only eight years before. Percy gave his true age: he had just celebrated his twenty-fifth birthday. Marie gilded the lily: she was only 17, but declared she was 18. After the wedding, Marie allowed herself no honeymoon. Two days later, she opened at Lowrey's music-hall in Dublin.

Marie and Percy set up home in Arlington Square, not far from her beloved Hoxton, but one distinct rung up the social ladder. While

Marie improved her lot, she was intent on not leaving her family behind. She made her mother give up work and moved her parents, brothers and sisters into a larger, more comfortable home in nearby Richmond Street. She bought new furniture, as well as a piano – acquired on the never-never. She also demonstrated an alarming enthusiasm for introducing some colour into the family's drab surroundings. A paint known as Aspinall's enamel was then all the rage, and so Marie set about painting the Richmond Street rooms different colours – one pink, another red, another blue, and so on. She was so impetuous that she rarely let the paint dry before moving furniture back in, and her family often found their beds stuck to the walls!

That Christmas, she was at two halls: the Oxford: '[her] dancing is marked by an ease which heightens its inherent value' (*Entr'acte* 4 February 1888), and the Middlesex: 'Marie Lloyd's songs and expert dances are deservedly popular'. (*Entr'acte* 28 January 1888) But by the spring of 1888 her engagements started decreasing ... because she was pregnant. On 19 May, seven months after she married, a daughter was born – Myria Matilda Victoria.

The work continued – the Foresters, the South London, the Royal Cambridge; and then there was a new venture – pantomime. Marie was hired by Sara Lane to appear at the Britannia in Hoxton. Mrs Lane, who owned the Brit, as it was called, was something of a local celebrity. Known, on account of her generosity, as the Queen of Hoxton, she insisted on appearing in her own shows. In panto, she was Principal Boy, wearing black silk tights, even when she was over seventy.

Pantomime then was a very different show from what it is now. The pantomime itself served merely as a prelude to the Harlequinade, in which all the traditional characters appeared – Columbine, Pantaloon and the rest. It all made for a long show, and so matinees began at midday and evening performances at seven. Charles Dickens attended one Britannia pantomime, and recalled in *The Uncommercial Traveller*: 'Before it was over, I felt as if I had been travelling for six weeks – going to India, say, by the Overland Mail.' (Dickens 1860)

Two of the Lupinos, a long-established family of acrobats, dancers and pantomime players, had married into Sara Lane's family; and so the show in which Marie appeared was laden with Lupinos. It was called *The Magic Dragon of the Demon Dell or the Search for the Mystic Thyme*. Marie played Princess Kristina. The show opened on Boxing Day 1888 and ran until the end of February 1889. It provided good theatrical experience for Marie, but, as she was to find out, her love of ad-libbing was not always welcomed by theatre managements.

Marie returned to the music-halls both in Brighton, where she appeared for a week with the black-faced singer G.H. Chirgwin, and in London, at the Canterbury, the Middlesex and, with Dan Leno and Little Tich, at the prestigious Empire in Leicester Square.

At about this time, moves were afoot to change the way in which the administration of London was conducted. Although no one then realized it, the changes would have a devastating effect on London's music-hall too.

Earlier in the nineteenth century, London was run in a somewhat ramshackle fashion. At one stage, no fewer than 300 organizations looked after the roads, the sewers, the lighting, the lunatic asylums, and so on. Some of the confusion was alleviated with the creation of a Metropolitan Board of Works. But everyone realized the real answer was to set up an overall authority – the London County Council, and the first election were held on 17 January 1889. One remarkable outcome was the number of teetotallers on the new body – a group of councillors so strict that they even refused their Chairman a civic entertainments allowance.

Of the Council committees that were formed, one – the Theatres and Music-Halls Committee – took over the job of licensing halls from the courts. The committee, elected in May 1889 comprised thirty members. The Chairman was Thomas Fardell, the son of a Canon of Ely and a barrister by profession. The music-hall world was given some idea of what was coming to them when the name of the vice-Chairman was announced – none other than George Russell, the Chairman of the National Vigilance Association. Worse still, Frederick Charrington had gained a place, as had George Lidgett, whose sister Mary was active in the NVA. In addition, Captain Edmund Verney, who represented Brixton, was sympathetic to the Association's principles.

The committee's main task was to ensure that places of entertainment were structurally safe. Its members insisted that, in addition, they intended to turn music-halls into havens of purity. No one made that clearer than another committee member, a prominent Methodist, John McDougall, who became known as MuckDougall. In a speech at the Rectory Road Congregational Church in Stoke Newington, he left no doubt about what he thought should be done to music-halls:

> It is possible for a music-hall entertainment to be conducted as to be harmless. There is no necessity to surround these amusements with great temptations to drink. The two things might be kept entirely separate. It is unfair that people should be attracted to those places to

seek amusements to have their moral sense stolen by the temptations by which they are surrounded when they get inside. The County Council has not decided to abolish these places, but to purify them. Amusements are necessary and are not necessarily degrading. It is only when they are associated with such temptations as are to be found in our music-halls that they fail. (*Era* 15 March 1890)

At Blackheath Literary and Debating Society he went one step further, suggesting the view that all songs should be considered by a censor before they were sung in public. 'However good the song might be at first, there is no doubt that, after repetition from time to time, the audience gets to know it very well and the desire of the artist is to please. Verse after verse is added and each verse becomes more spicy than the last.' (*Era* 21 February 1891)

McDougall said he had stayed at one hall until 11.30 p.m. 'As the audience got more drink in them, the performance got coarser and more lewd ... The people got into a noisy state, ready to receive anything and some of the songs were beyond description.' (*Era* 21 February 1891)

If anyone were by now in any doubt, McDougall stressed his sense of mission to the Pleasant Sunday Afternoon Society at Canning Town Congregational Church: '[The County Council] only wants to secure decency and propriety – not to stop amusement. The Lord Chamberlain – a highly salaried official – looks after morality in rich people's amusements – the theatres – and the Council is only trying to do the same thing with regard to the amusements of the poor.' (*Era* 19 March 1892)

At the committee's meeting in October 1889, McDougall showed how he meant to impose his views on others. He opposed an application for a licence for the Rosemary Branch, a hall in Camberwell, on account of two songs, 'They Do Try Hard' and 'A Way They Have in the Navy'; a dancer in short skirts; a ventriloquist he found objectionable, and a black man in drag. He objected to Crowder's Music Hall in Greenwich because of two songs, 'Why Don't They Do It?' and 'Not at all the Silly Girl you took me for' by George Lashwood, a highly popular comedian then at the start of his career, and a sketch called 'The Doctor's Boy', which he found indecent. He also made a fuss over the licence for the Canterbury about a sketch entitled 'The Bewitched Curate', in which a clergyman, 'enamoured of a young lady, showed how shocked he was by her behaviour'. Despite his remonstrations, all the halls were granted their licences.

Although these attempts at censorship caused an outcry among music-hall audiences, others organized their support for the Council. A few days after that committee meeting, a rally was held at St James'

Hall, chaired by Bishop Temple. He told the meeting that it was the duty of the authorities to forbid 'any kind of entertainment, which distinctly suggests ... what is not consistent with Christian purity.' (*Era* 1889) A prominent Methodist, the Reverend Hugh Price Hughes, who was also a member of the National Vigilance Association, said the time had come when 'obscenity in places of public amusement ... must unhesitatingly [be] put down'. (*Era* 1889) The Bishop of Bedford put down a motion rejoicing in the 'determination of the ... committee ... to reform the music-halls of London.' (*Era* 1889) But, when someone tried to move an amendment, there was several minutes' uproar. When he was eventually able to make himself heard, Bishop Temple ruled that no amendment was admissible as the meeting had been called purely to support the committee!

George Bernard Shaw once expressed the hope that the London County Council would deal with the halls better than the courts had. 'I am convinced that music-halls, when they are freed from the censorship of Middlesex magistrates and their like, will do more to educate the people artistically than all the nimminy-pimminy concerts in the world.' (Laurence 1965) In that respect, at least, the Great Man was wrong.

# Chapter 4

## 1890

# MARIE'S AMERICAN DÉBUT

At this stage, none of this moralizing had anything to do with Marie, for although she was winning acclaim on all sides, she had yet to make a really big impact. For one thing, she was still singing songs like 'Oh Jeremiah'. One reviewer neatly summed up her standing: 'Marie Lloyd is a good hard-working little lady, who invariably looks nice, sings agreeably and dances well. She lacks only one thing – new songs.' (*Entr'acte* 31 December 1887)

In 1890, that was to change. The year began badly with the birth of a stillborn child, but Marie suffered no ill-effects. The big opportunity she had been waiting for came after she had met the song-writer George le Brunn. She pinpointed the start of her stardom at a Sunday lunch party:

> There was a convivial little gathering in progress and George le Brunn sat at the piano, playing anything and everything. I said to him in the way of a joke about something that was going on 'Oh, wink the other eye, George' and he repeated the words playing a sort of accompaniment. Well, it just occurred to us 'What a good song that would make'. (*Era* 28 October 1893)

Le Brunn wrote the melody on the spot. The words were supplied by W.T. Lytton, a schoolmaster-cum-lyric writer.

Say, boys, whatever do you mean
When you wink the other eye?
Why, when you tell us where've you been,
Do you wink the other eye?
You preach your wives such stories
You can tell them just a few
'Just met an old acquaintance'

Or 'The train was overdue'
Then you wink the other eye.

Say, boys, is it quite the thing?
Say, should we let you have your fling?
Oh, when you've got us on the string?
Then you wink the other eye!

Le Brunn was well known for the speed with which he worked. His main collaborator, John P. Harrington, almost begrudged him the talent.

Any old place and time, George could compose songs as easily and deftly as another man might write a letter. A rapid glance at the lyric, a grunted 'This in six-eight time, eh?' and, after my nod of acquiescence, presto! His fluent pen would positively fly over the sheet of music paper and the melody was written ere you had time to gasp 'Gee-whizz!'

Seldom, if ever, was so much as a note altered afterwards and never once was the piano touched, until the melody was completed. I have known him to reel off half a dozen melodies in this fashion and some of our most popular songs were composed in ten or fifteen minutes. Foolishly, at first, I was a little indignant that George earned his money apparently so easily, whilst the lyric took me perhaps an hour or two to write. (*Era* 12 October 1922)

He also had praise for Marie:

I first saw Marie on the stage when she was a very young girl ... and I prophesied even then that she was destined to become a star. How great a one and how considerable a part I should have in helping her reach that dizzy height I little knew then.

When I first wrote for her, she had an almost uncanny gift of visualising herself right inside the 'skin' of a song, if I may use the term, and her 'underlining' of any tricky or uncommon points in a number always made it a keen pleasure to me to take Marie anything a bit out of the beaten track. She grasped my every intention in the lines so readily that it was a sheer delight to listen to her trying a new song of mine over. (*Era* 9 November 1922)

'Wink the Other Eye' was a big success, which put Marie at the top of the bill, where she stayed for the next thirty-two years. It set the seal on Marie's individual style. She had no need for a vulgar lyric: she could make a point much more cleverly with a wink, a smile, a certain look, a flick of her dress. Her mastery of these mannerisms infuriated her critics. How could they accuse her of being vulgar when the words of her songs sounded innocent enough?

The music-hall impresario Don Ross, who saw Marie perform more than 100 times, wrote:

> No one could put into a song what Marie did with her wink, her nod, her pauses and her lovely smile. She had tremendous repose and this accentuated the slightest movement of her hand or facial expression. She had a wonderful knack of making a quite innocent line sound suggestive, just as in later years, Max Miller did. I am sure Marie could have recited the 23rd Psalm and make it sound indecent – without intention. (Ross, undated)

Like all music-hall successes, 'Wink The Other Eye' had its immediate spin-off – a piece of nonsense called 'Listen with the Right Ear', the work of le Brunn and George Ware:

> Listen with your right ear to all you wish to hear
> Keep your left ear closed and you'll have no cause to fear
> You keep your right ear open and the left lug shut
> Then you'll hear all that suits you, that's an old chestnut.

Time and time again, Harrington and le Brunn provided Marie with hit songs. Another she bought in 1890 was 'The Wrong Man':

> One night, my beau was rather late in calling round for me
> And, when I heard a loud rat-tat, thinks I 'That must be he'.
> So, I rushed to the passage and no chance of courtship missing
> All in the dark I kissed him twice – then found that I'd been kissing
>
> The wrong man! the wrong man! Wasn't it awful rum?
> The wrong man! the wrong man! Oh, Jerusalum!
> I never was in such a plight before
> Pity me if you can
> I thought I should fall
> I'd given them all
> To the wrong, wrong man.

Although it's now hard to see anything indelicate in 'Wink the Other Eye' or 'The Wrong Man', both songs did poke fun at infidelity, albeit in its mildest form. The purity brigade marked Marie out as a woman to watch. But music-hall managements were determined to keep on the right side of the new authorities. Programmes at the Middlesex, where Marie appeared that summer, carried this note: 'The proprietors ... will be obliged to anyone who will inform them or their manager of any suggestive or offensive word or action upon the stage that may have escaped the notice of the management.'

For the moment, they had no need to worry. In a report to the

Theatres and Music-Halls Committee, a Council inspector described 'the character of performance' at the Middlesex as 'a good variety entertainment'. Meanwhile, reviewers continued to heap praise on Marie. The *Era* commented: 'Miss Marie Lloyd ... must be congratulated on the big success of her song (When You) Wink The Other Eye ... Miss Lloyd once used to depend on her dancing for her success, but she is wise to relinquish such exhausting work in favour of serio-comic singing.'

Her act now consisted of three songs: first 'The Wrong Man', then 'Oh Jeremiah' and 'Wink The Other Eye' to finish with. Like other entertainers in demand, she played a number of halls each evening: The Paragon at 9 p.m., the Canterbury at 9.45 p.m., the Alhambra at 10.15 p.m. and the Charing Cross at 10.45 p.m. It meant a mad dash from one hall to another in a brougham.

Up to now, Marie had been earning about £10 a week. At the height of her new-found fame, George Ware fixed eight weeks' work for her in New York at a fee of £50 a week. On 20 September 1890 she set sail.

Music-hall in America (and, contrary to popular opinion, it was music-hall; vaudeville came later) developed in much the same way as in Britain. Concert saloons, in which earthy entertainment was staged for a male clientele, started springing up in New York in the 1850s. By the time Marie arrived, the three managers who had cornered the market were a former black-face minstrel, circus ringmaster, clown and comic singer, Tony Pastor, and, working in partnership, John Koster and Adam Bial. All three booked entertainers from England through agents. Pastor was particularly reliant on them, as a phobia of deep water prevented him travelling to England. He was a resourceful manager, though. He was the first to introduce New York audiences to Jenny Hill, who was as successful on the halls in the 1870s and 1880s as Marie was in the 1890s. He was so concerned that his audience might not understand her Cockney patter that he distributed specially prepared dictionaries. But it was Koster and Bial who lured Marie across the Atlantic first. They had started out as brewers. So, in 1879, when they opened Koster and Bial's Music-Hall on Twenty-third Street, they were chiefly interested in selling alcohol. It was a rough-and-ready place, and to evade a law forbidding the sale of drink in theatres, the partners fixed up a large folding fan, instead of a curtain, across the front of their small stage.

Marie scored a hit there, although she was angered to find another entertainer singing her songs – the very mistake she had made in Britain at the start of her career. Now that the boot was on the other foot, Marie reacted with characteristic indignation:

Pinch? They'd pinch your eye-teeth, if they caught you napping! Know what they do? They hear you in New York. Then, they get someone to take down your best song in shorthand and another fellow to dot down the melody. Next thing you hear, they go to Chicago or somewhere like that, announce 'An impression of the Popular English Star, Marie Lloyd' and sing your whole darn song and copy your dress and all your actions into the bargain. Then, when you get to Chicago yourself and sing the same song, you leave your audience cold! They say you're not a bit like your pincher's impression of Marie Lloyd! How's that for rubbing it in? And the blessed law of America won't allow you to stop these daylight robbers, even if you want to! (*Era* 28 December 1922)

Even so, the main American theatrical paper, the *New York Clipper*, reported that Marie had made 'legions of friends'; the *New York Herald* called her 'a distinct success', while the *New York Sun* described her as 'the best representative of the music-halls New York has seen'. By the time she sailed back to a fog-bound Liverpool, she had reason to be well pleased with her American début.

# Chapter 5

## 1891

# SUCCESS AT DRURY LANE

Back in London, it was time to move again – Marie, Percy and Myria to Graham Road, Dalston, and the family (naturally not far away) to Powerscroft Road, Clapton; but not for long. The next move brought all the family under one roof – in an old-fashioned house with a big garden and stables in Lewisham Road, New Cross. For the Woods it was the last word in luxury. The family – all of them stagestruck – loved enjoying themselves. Their main amusement was play-acting and dressing up. Alice wrote:

> Marie used to put us all into tights and, donning the same costume herself, padded with preposterous muscles, would lead what she called the Keleino Family of Acrobats, balancing us on her shoulders and going through antics, which set mother and father in roars of laughter – until one of us fell with a crash and laughter gave place to yells of pain. (*Lloyds Sunday News* 1922)

Although they were living in Lewisham (and it was not long before they moved again – to leafy Brixton), they were clearly not going to change their ways. To Marie, one of the greatest treats was the Sunday tradition of a tea of winkles. But winkles were not to be found in Lewisham. So, every week, Marie took her pony and trap up to the Old Kent Road to collect supplies.

A meeting early in 1891 gave Marie the chance to build on her stardom. Augustus Harris, the greatest showman of his time, wanted her for pantomime. And Harris usually got what he wanted.

In 1879, the Theatre Royal, Drury Lane, had closed because of financial problems. Harris desperately wanted to take it over. Although he was only 27, his bid was taken seriously. He was told that, if he could raise £3,000, the theatre was his. There was only one

# DRURY LANE PANTOMIME.

MISS MARIE LLOYD AND LITTLE (VERY LITTLE) TICH.

problem: his capital amounted to £3 15s. One of the unsuccessful contenders immediately promised him £2,000, if he could find the rest. He found only £750, but that was accepted. Harris moved into the Theatre Royal and made it the National Theatre of its day.

He thought big: his production of *Carmen* had real bulls; his portrayal of the Derby had horses running at full gallop, and he staged ships sinking in dreadful storms and trains being wrecked. He thought nothing of spending as much as £5,000 on a show. As if Drury Lane were not enough, he took on the Royal Opera House in Covent Garden, too. 'If opera is dead,' he told a friend, 'I intend to bury it decently. If it can be revived, I intend to give it a new lease of life.' (*The Times* 23 June 1896)

His penchant for the grandiose extended to the pantomimes he staged. They were recognized as the most spectacular since George Conquest's at the Grecian. Harris's passion was processions, depicting famous cities, health resorts, the Kings and Queens of England – whatever took his fancy. Five hundred people on the stage at one time was nothing, although it did provide him with a quandary over *Ali Baba and the Forty Thieves*. To Harris, forty was clearly not enough, but he solved the problem by allowing each thief ten subordinates. In that way, he achieved more than four hundred thieves. It's hardly surprising that Harris's pantomimes often ended at one in the morning!

When Harris asked Marie to be in the 1891/92 pantomime at Drury Lane, she affected not to be impressed.

> I was intensely excited and flattered by the offer, but I am thankful to say that I was actress enough not to allow my excitement to betray itself.
>
> 'To Drury Lane?' I repeated nonchalantly, the while pretending to be wrapped in thought. 'Do you mean the Middlesex Music Hall?'
>
> 'No ... I mean Drury Lane theatre.'
>
> 'I don't think I know it,' I said, puckering my brows.
>
> 'Not know it?' cried the manager, not a little bit enraged. 'You must know it. It's the large building at the centre of the Lane, with the soldiers and the sentry-boxes outside.'
>
> 'Oh, is that a theatre?' I inquired, pretending to be intensely astonished. 'I always thought it was a barracks.' (*The Strand* February 1912)

Marie had Drury Lane to look forward to. In the meantime, it was back to the halls. The routine this time was: Collins, 8.50 p.m.; the Oxford 9.45 p.m.; the Pavilion 10.15 p.m. and the South London 10.50 p.m.

There were two new songs, too – 'Never Let A Chance Go By' and

'Don't Laugh', both composed by George le Brunn. The lyrics of 'Don't Laugh' were by Richard Morton:

> If a nice young curate's mashed on you, Don't Laugh.
> For a curate can be good and true, Don't Smile
> He's the mildest of all mild young men
> Be on your best behaviour then
> And though he must be in by ten
> Don't say anything to shock him.

In February 1891, a new comedian arrived on the scene. He was Albert Chevalier, best remembered for 'My Old Dutch'. Up to then, he had been an actor in the so-called legitimate theatre, but he wanted to try his hand at the halls. An engagement was arranged at the London Pavilion, but he received little encouragement. The playwright Sir Arthur Pinero told him he would be ruined for life if he ever appeared in such a 'dog kennel' as the Pavilion. (Roberts 1927) Understandably, he was a nervous wreck by the time the night arrived. But Marie stood in the wings, ready to prompt him. Dressed as a coster, he sang three songs – all of them of a style quite new to music-hall audiences. But he was unaccustomed to the rowdiness of a music-hall, and as he came off that night, he was dejected.

> 'I can't stand it!'
> 'What's the matter?' asked the stage manager.
> 'The horrible din. The awful row they have been making. I have never played in such a row in my life.'
> 'Row,' exclaimed Marie ... 'Why tonight they are quiet as bloody church mice!' (Roberts 1927)

Noise or no noise, Chevalier was, literally, an overnight success. Later in his career, he would be able to lend Marie the sort of support she had given him on his début in the halls.

By now, Marie was pulling the crowds in. One night at the Tivoli, she was ready to try out a new song. Most of the audience were not actually in the theatre, but in the saloon bar, which was thick with cigar smoke. It was a scene the journalist J.B. Booth witnessed time after time.

> 'Marie's number!' cries a voice; glasses were put down; and the big room empties in a trice. We elbow our way to the promenade at the back of the circle and lean our arms on the partition dividing it from the back row of seats to watch.
> The orchestra has struck up a typical Marie Lloyd number – jaunty, debonair, catchy – and the house waits in silence. Then, from the

wings, comes a little fair-haired woman, blue-eyed, with an indescribable friendly smile and there is a roar of welcome from ceiling to floor.

A cheery nod of recognition and salute, a tiny wave of the hand and 'Our Marie' begins.

The song? Nothing in particular. As with most of the great artists of the halls, it is simply a vehicle, but, make no mistake, trite as it may seem, there is method in it. It is cleverly designed for its purpose and it fulfils that purpose better than a more aesthetic composition could do.

So, the song is nothing in particular. The singer is everything.

Watch the play of the hands, the eyes, the controlled and perfect gesture; listen to the intonation of the tritest words and, in spite of all attempts at criticism and dissection, you yield yourself to the artist.

In some indescribable way, she has gathered her audience to her; they are hers, to do with as she pleases ... 'We're all pals together,' she seems to say, 'and, strictly as pals, what do you think of this?' (Booth 1943)

That scene was repeated again and again in 1891. For Marie was trying out plenty of new songs – 'Actions Speak Louder Than Words' by George le Brunn and Harry Leighton; 'I Was Slapped'; 'The Trumpet Call'; 'How Dare You Come to London'; and 'I Say'. Another song, 'That Was Before My Time', by T.W. Connor, was intended to show that Marie did not mean to be the prim little girl of previous generations.

That was before my time, you know, a long, long time ago
For girls to wear dresses their figures to show
Was reckoned an awful crime
They went to tea meetings along with their Ma's
And filled up their time darning socks for their Pa's
Well, it may have been so, but it happened you know
Before my time.

Yet another new song was 'Madame Du Van', the joint work of the comedian Tom Costello and another prolific writer, Joseph Tabrar, the man responsible for Vesta Victoria's biggest success, 'Daddy Wouldn't Buy Me a Bow-wow'. It was a bit of a dig at theatre women with social aspirations. Two years previously, one half of the Sisters Bilton, Belle Bilton, had become Lady Clancarty; and it was a practice that was to continue (vide Jose Collins, Gertie Millar, Adele Astaire, Tilly Losch and others):

I suppose you've heard of Madame du Van
Well, if you have not heard of her, you can
She's a lady far from shady
Though her father keeps a bak'd potato can, Ta-ra-ra.
On the stage, she acts a little bit
Best adapted to the gallery and pit
People hiss her, actors kiss her
But no-one seems to care about her wit. Ta-ra-ra.

On the stage, she's Madame du Van
At home, her name is Mary Ann
Silks and satins now she can't afford
She didn't want to be the rage
She only went upon the stage
In hopes of wedding a Viscount or a Lord

In an interview, Marie described how hard it was to find the right song.

There's a good deal of picking and choosing to be done first. You can't say that you want a new song and just buy it. I ... buy an immense number that I cannot sing. I have quite a large collection of songs that I shall probably never sing. You may take it that one has to buy ten songs before one finds a really good one. (*Era* October 1893)

Another of the songs she launched in 1891 was a sequel to one of Chevalier's first successes – the 'Coster's Serenade'. Music-hall stars loved parodies and answer songs. The lyric of the 'Serenade', which Chevalier wrote himself, screamed out to be parodied:

Oh! 'arriet, I'm waiting, waiting for you, my dear
Oh, 'arriet. I'm waiting, waiting alone out here
When that moon shall cease to shine
False will be his 'eart of mine
I'm bound to go on lovin' yer, my dear, d'ye 'ear?

Before long, it was being hummed and whistled all over London. That gave Jenny Hill the opportunity to commission ' 'Arriet's Answer' from le Brunn and another of his collaborators, A.J. Morris. And Marie sang something similar, ' 'Arriet's Reply'.

Marie appeared mostly in London in 1891. During the summer she embarked on a short provincial tour which took her to Liverpool, Cardiff and Manchester. But, by the start of August, she was back in the West End. The National Vigilance Association continued to monitor the standards of decency on display at the halls, although its campaign took something of a knock when Captain Verney, one of its supporters on the LCC, appeared in court charged with aiding and abetting the procurement for an immoral purpose of a teenage girl called Nellie Baskett. He was sentenced to a year's imprisonment.

One afternoon in November, the music-hall profession staged a tribute to Marie in the form of a benefit concert at the Oxford. It marked the first public appearance of Marie junior, aged three-and-a-half.

For Marie senior, the main event of the year was the Drury Lane pantomime, *Humpty Dumpty or the Yellow Dwarf and the Fair One with the Golden Locks*. Marie played the Fair One with the Golden Locks. By the time the pantomime season came round, Gus Harris had been knighted for his work as an Under-Sheriff of London. He enjoyed public life. He also sat on the LCC, doing his best to combat the anti-music-hall lobby.

As if he were not already busy enough, he also wrote *Humpty Dumpty* in conjunction with Harry Nicholls, a comic who had played opposite Herbert Campbell at the Grecian pantos. There were, in all, eleven scenes before the Grand Transformation that led into the Harlequinade that featured an old panto favourite – Harry Payne as clown. Harry Nicholls believed in keeping the script up-to-date. Some evenings, he wrote new verses, based on the day's newspaper stories. For *Humpty Dumpty*, Harris gathered together a particularly strong cast. There was Little Tich, dancing in boots almost as long as he was tall – and that was only four feet six. He was Humpty. Then there were Herbert Campbell and Dan Leno, who, as the King and Queen of Hearts, were teamed as a double act for the first time. It was the start of a partnership that was to dominate Drury Lane pantomimes for many years to come. Indeed, the way in which the two men played off each other laid the groundwork for many of the comic double acts that succeeded them. For a start, Campbell and Leno looked funny. At nineteen stone, Campbell became the perfect foil for sad little Dan Leno.

By now, many regarded Marie as the funniest woman on the halls and Dan as the funniest man. The critic Max Beerbohm tried to sum up Dan's appeal:

> The moment Dan Leno skipped upon the stage, we were aware that here was a man utterly unlike anyone else we had seen. Despite the rusty top hat and broken umbrella and red nose of tradition, here was a creature apart, radiating an ethereal essence all his own. He compelled us not to take our eyes off him, not to miss a word that he said ... That face so tragic ... yet ever liable to relax its mouth into a sudden wide grin and to screw up its eyes over some little triumph ... that poor little battered personage, so 'put upon', yet so plucky with his squeaking

voice and his sweeping gestures; bent but not broken; faint but pursuing. (Beerbohm 1954)

Inevitably, the script of 'Humpty Dumpty' now sounds flat and unfunny. In the third of eleven scenes, Marie insisted she would not marry.

| | |
|---|---|
| King: | Why don't you wish to wed? |
| Princess: | It seem such nonsense. |
| Queen: | What was that you said? |
| King: | You *may* be happy. |
| Princess: | May be – I admit. |
| Queen: | Look at your pa and me! |
| Princess: | Yes, that's just it. |

Needless to say, she did fall in love, and Humpty tried to make off with her. But everything ended happily. All through, the show was laced with currently popular songs, including 'Never Introduce Your Donah to a Pal', and one of Marie's:

Say, boys, if it's quite the thing
As I'm going to wed a king
May I be allowed to sing
That I'll wink the other eye.

The show opened on Boxing Day. There was not a spare seat in the house. Marie had the plum part in the best panto in the country for which Gus Harris was paying her £100 a week. She had come a long way from the Britannia Theatre, Hoxton.

# Chapter 6
## 1892
# PROVINCIAL HALLS
# AND CHARGES OF IMMORALITY

Each night, Marie's lines about the futility of marriage must have rung unpleasantly true. Her marriage to Percy Courtenay was going wrong. According to her dresser, Bella Orchard, Courtenay objected to the fact that he and Marie never had time to themselves. Their home attracted a constant flow of visitors. During the week, Marie was surrounded by her music-hall friends, and on Sunday she kept open house, serving food and drink to anyone who called – from midday to midnight. Perhaps Marie's rapidly increasing income made Courtenay jealous. She allowed him three pounds a week pocket money, but he still ran up debts which he expected her to settle.

Whatever the difficulties, there was no excusing an outburst which occurred less than three weeks into the run of *Humpty Dumpty*. Marie was resting in her dressing-room, and, for some reason, Courtenay, who was with her, turned violent. It was said he accused her of leading an immoral life. In any case, Marie denied it. But Courtenay was not to be placated; taking down a sword that was hanging in the room, he threatened to cut her throat. As she tried to get out, he kicked her in the back and on the leg. Marie went straight to Bow Street police station, where she saw a magistrate. Within a few days, Courtenay was in the dock, charged with assault. He was bound over to keep the peace for six months.

As it turned out, Marie had no reason to spend any more time with him than she wanted to. Once the pantomime had finished early in April, George Ware had work booked for her for the rest of the year: first, a fortnight at the Grand Theatre, Liverpool, then seven weeks at halls in London. This time, the routine was: the Oxford 8.30 p.m.; the Metropolitan 9.05 p.m.; the Trocadero 9.35 p.m.; the Alhambra

10.10 p.m., and the South London Palace 10.50 p.m.

She then embarked on her first extended tour of provincial halls. Given that her only means of travel was train, steamer and brougham, it was a taxing schedule. But it set the pattern for future years. This is how Marie spent the summer:

| | |
|---|---|
| June: | Derby Castle, Douglas |
| | Empire, Swansea |
| July: | Gaiety, Birmingham |
| | Empire, Newport |
| | Palace, Manchester |
| August: | Grand, Liverpool |
| | Empire, Cardiff |
| September: | Gaiety, Glasgow |
| | Alhambra, Brighton |

Glasgow presented a challenge to every comic, and audiences at the Gaiety were renowned for giving newcomers a hostile reception. But Marie won them over. One local paper said she had made 'the biggest success ever known at the theatre'. (*Glasgow Evening News*) Another said she had 'the fortune to be ... a thorough actress'. (*Glasgow Evening Times*) Yet another praised her for her 'handsome presence' and 'fascinating manner'. (*North British Daily Mail*).

There were, of course, new songs. At first sight, 'Whacky Whack Whack', written by George Ware, looked a treat for disciplinarians. The sheet music showed her as a schoolgirl surrounded by canes:

I'm a little schoolgirl and I love to play
With the boys at marbles I could play all day
I've got a little brother, We all call him Jack
And if late to school we get, Whacky Whack Whack

Another song was packed with Cockney slang – 'G'arn Away', written by E.W. Rogers, the composer of 'Ask a Policeman':

Just because I'm a slimy girl, yer takes me for a jay
But you bet your Sunday collar that I'm fly
And a chap as thinks he's a-goin' to lark about with me
Stands a chance of gittin' dotted in the eye.
T'other night a bloke as drives an 'orse for Pickford says to me
I've got lots of 'oof, so come and have a supper and a spree
He says What'll yer 'ave? Why h'oysters, Jim says, I but blow my eyes
When 'e says that whelks was best, yer know! I turns to 'im and cries
G'arn away, do you take me for a silly?
G'arn away, do you take me for a jay?
Yer think yer've got me for a mug – well I'm sure
Strike me up a mulberry, what d'yer take me for, eh?

(Glossary: *slimy* = deceitful; *jay* = simpleton; *oof* = money.)

The *Era* commented:

> 'Miss Lloyd gets to the lower deeps of gutter slang. It would be difficult
> to interpret the meaning of such a phrase as 'strike me up a mulberry' ...
> We will not attempt its elucidation.'

Another song was a response to Charles Coborn's big hit, 'The Gal
Wot Lost Her Bloke at Monte Carlo', written by Charles Deane and
George le Brunn's brother, Thomas. But the two songs with which she
was having most success were 'Twiggy Voo', written by Richard
Morton and George le Brunn, and 'Oh Mr Porter' by both le Brunns.

Capitalizing on the looks and smiles that made 'Wink The Other
Eye' so popular, 'Twiggy Voo' gave Marie an ever greater chance to
leave alternative meanings to the audience's imagination. One verse
ran:

> When a girl goes to be wed
> She is nearly off her head
> And, upon my word, she don't know what to do
> She is frightened, for, O Lor'
> She's never done such things before
> Twiggy voo? my boys Twiggy voo?

'Oh Mr Porter' provided her with her most durable success:

> Oh Mr Porter, what shall I do?
> I want to go to Birmingham and they're taking me on to Crewe
> Send me back to London as quickly as you can
> Oh Mr Porter, what a silly girl I am.

The song was – in Marie's words – a stormer. But it caused a division
of opinion among two distinguished writers. Of all Marie's songs, Max
Beerbohm knew which he liked best:

> Oh, Mr Porter was always my favourite – the flurry, the frantic distress
> of it: I wanted to go to Birmin*gham* and they're taking me on to Crewe.
> The accent was always on the last syllable of Birmingham, which
> helped the rhythm. Rhythm was one of her strong points. She had an
> exquisitely sensitive ear, impeccable phrasing and timing. But sheer joy
> of living was always her strongest point of all. Even in the agony of
> being taken on to Crewe, Marie ... was bursting with rapture and made
> us partakers of it. (Beerbohm 1954)

But George Bernard Shaw, at that time the music critic of *The World*, thought otherwise:

> Miss Marie Lloyd, like all the brightest stars of music-hall, has an exceptionally quick ear for both pitch and rhythm. Her intonation and the lilt of her songs are alike perfect. Her step-dancing is pretty; and her command of coster-girls' patois is complete. Why, then, does not someone write humorous songs for her? Twiggy voo is low and silly; and Oh Mr Porter, though very funnily sung, is not itself particularly funny. A humorous rhymester of any genius could easily make it so. (Shaw, 19 October 1892)

Shaw knew Mrs Ormiston Chant – indeed, he partly modelled *Candida* on her – but he did not share her views. Whilst he thought Marie's songs were silly, she thought them immoral. It's said that, at some stage, Mrs Chant stood up in a theatre where Marie was singing and protested, though it's not known which theatre. In fact, uncertainty surrounds some of the best legends involving Marie Lloyd. Time and again the story has been told that Marie was summoned before some sort of committee to answer allegations that she was singing a dirty song; that she appeared before them; that she sang the song in question without any elaboration; that she won the committee's approval, and that she then sang some guileless ballad like 'Come Into The Garden, Maud' as lasciviously as she dared. It is a good story, but it does not bear close examination.

Some say the song complained of was 'Twiggy Voo'; others insist it was 'Maid of London Ere We Part', whilst still more claim it was a song either entitled or containing the line 'She sits among the cabbages and leeks' (or, possibly, 'peas'). But the only song to contain a line similar to that was 'Mucking about the Garden' (or at least, some versions of it), which Leslie Sarony wrote in 1929 – seven years after Marie's death.

The story has a group of puritans or a Watch Committee demanding to see her. Now, the National Vigilance Association, the most active anti-music-hall organization of the time, did not have the power to issue orders to an artiste in this way; and it is hardly likely that Marie would have volunteered to appear before them. Perhaps it was the LCC's Theatres and Music-Halls Committee. The committee was not empowered to order entertainers to appear before its members, but, occasionally, music-hall managers who had received complaints about certain artistes would take them with them to licensing meetings to try to convince councillors they were cleaner than their reputations. There is no evidence that Marie ever attended such a meeting, although in 1897, she told reporters that the LCC had dissected one of her songs and had found it harmless. She may have come face to face with her opponents, but it cannot be proved. It is a good story, though, and it will go on being told.

By the end of 1892 Marie had no reason to be concerned about what either Shaw or Mrs Ormiston Chant thought of her. Gus Harris thought enough of her to have booked her for her second Drury Lane pantomime.

# Chapter 7

## 1893

# LITTLE RED RIDING HOOD
# AND POLLY PERKINS

It was a different title (and something of a mouthful, too): *Little Bo-Peep, Little Red Riding Hood and Hop O' My Thumb*, but, when it came to the cast, Harris wanted the same mixture as before: Marie as Little Red Riding Hood; Little Tich as Hop o' my Thumb; Dan Leno as Daddy Thumb, and Herbert Campbell as Goody Thumb. Ada Blanche played Little Boy Blue. Harris, this time in collaboration with Wilton Jones, wrote fourteen scenes, encompassing a procession of twenty-nine well-known nursery rhymes and fairy tales and a parade of twenty-one sports.

The script seemed rather livelier, although the audience needed a quick grasp of puns. In the wood, Marie and Miss Blanche had this convoluted exchange:

Ada: Red Riding Hood, in pose so fond and true
    I as a pro-pose this day to you
    Oh, Marie (marry) me.
Marie: Don't make me (Blanche) with fear
    I feel that I must cry, Oh, tear, Oh tear
    And Ma's not here.
Ada: No, Ma's not between us
    I want no Mars (Ma's) with us, my little Venus.

After Marie had been saved from the wolf, 'Oh Mr Porter' was sung with a special pantomime lyric:

Oh, Mr Boy Blue, what shall we do?
We've captured both the wolves and now we'll take 'em to a zoo
Off they'll go to London; it isn't very far
Oh, you pair of duffers, what silly wolves you are.

47

DIRECTOR OF MUSIC-HALL, TO POPULAR ARTIST:—"WE SHALL BE VERY GLAD T
HAVE YOU ON OUR SIDE, MARIE; BUT YOU WILL BE GOOD, WON'T YOU?"

Harry Payne's Harlequinade again brought the whole phantasmagoria to a climax.

Marie followed the panto run with another season of London halls – the Oxford, the Empire, the Cambridge, the Canterbury and the Paragon – and two new songs: 'Mischief' by George and Thomas le Brunn and 'No, 'Arry, Don't Ask Me to Marry', on which George le Brunn collaborated with Harry Castling:

No, 'Arry, don't ask me to marry
Oblige me and let me be
I've got my mother, my sister and brother at home depending on me
There's the ring you gave me a year ago today
Take it back, 'twill remind you of me when you're miles away.

Then, from June to September, there was another provincial tour:

| | |
|---|---|
| June: | Folly, Manchester |
| | Gaiety, Birmingham, |
| July: | Gaiety, Glasgow |
| | Empire, Newcastle |
| | Derby Castle, Douglas |
| August: | Barnards, Chatham |
| | Empire, Portsmouth. |

Once again, Marie was anxious to publicize her reception in Glasgow: ' ... a great favourite here' (*Glasgow Evening News*); ' ... received with cheers, again and again renewed' (*Glasgow Evening Times*).

There was no break before she began another London season. She did, though, find time to be interviewed by one of the *Era*'s journalists. She ranged over a variety of subjects, including her costumes and her expenses:

I'm going to let you into a secret about my dresses. I make 'em all myself, every one. No, I tell a story. There's one I did not make – one with accordion pleats. But all the others are my own design and my own manufacture. Now, if you'd come up yesterday afternoon, you'd have found us all busy. Jenny Hill was here. I wear very pretty dresses, don't I? ... Of course, they come cheaper than if I bought them. But still they cost money. Lot of expenses? Yes, you're right there. When you come to reckon the cost of your songs, your dresses, your brougham, agent's fees and tips, it makes a hole in a good salary, I can tell you. But nobody seems to think of that – especially the Income Tax.

Marie's expenses also included acts of extraordinary generosity to the people she grew up with. Although she made no mention of it during the interview, she had bought 200 pairs of boots to be distributed among the poor of Hoxton.

During the *Era* interview, Marie also expressed her disapproval of the work of the Theatres and Music-Halls Committee, hinting that she may have already clashed with its members:

> Marie Lloyd enters into a long and interesting discourse on the comic song, its ethics and its characteristics. She cannot, she declares, understand the process by which the official and other censors of the music-hall arrive at their conclusions. They will see harm where none is intended ... They will complacently accept a questionable ditty. Miss Marie Lloyd, with a peal of laughter, recalls her challenge to a certain eminent authority. She undertook to sing nothing but 'Home Sweet Home' and lyrics of that class, provided she received a guarantee that her audience should be as morally unimpeachable as her songs. 'And was your challenge accepted, Miss Lloyd?' asks the unsophisticated interviewer. But Miss Lloyd, with an irrelevant remark about 'winking the other eye', proceeds to the question of publishing comic songs.

Here we have the possible truth behind the anecdote about Marie being called before a committee of 'puritans': that she issued a challenge to someone over the way she sang her songs, but that the challenge was not taken up.

Marie had some more new songs for her London season, which took her to the Metropolitan, the Canterbury, the Cambridge, the Empire, the Oxford, the Eastern Empire and English Sebrights. One was 'Same Thing' by E. W. Rogers:

> A proposal to a girl's the same in high degree or low
> Though the swell says 'Lady Maude, be mine, dost marm my passion's glow'
> When the coster says 'My 'and and 'eart, I offers, Sal, What O'
> Same thing, don't you know, same thing.

Another saucier song played on the popularity of Marie's wink – 'Silly Fool', written by Harrington and le Brunn:

> My sister's got a fellow and he calls each day
> Silly fool! Silly fool!
> If I am in the parlour, then he says 'Run and play!'
> Silly fool! Silly fool!
> I says 'No! Not for nuffin'! 'cause I thinks I've got a claim
> Then he gives me a shilling not to spoil his little game
> But that room's got a key-hole – I enjoys it just the same
> Silly fool! Silly fool!

In December, Marie staged a skit at a benefit concert in her honour at the Canterbury. She took a swipe – then harmlessly racial – at a group of dancers from the former West African state of Dahomey.

They called themselves the Dahomey Warriors. They were appearing at the Oxford. According to a review in the *Era*, they gave 'bridal and fetish' dances. Marie parodied them as the Amazing Worriers, in which – with the help of Little Tich and George Robey – she played Gumma, the Amazon Queen.

From then on, it was downhill all the way to her third Drury Lane pantomime – this time *Robinson Crusoe* – on which Harris again collaborated with Harry Nicholls. Once more, Harris took no chances with his stars. Ada Blanche appeared again this time in the title role. Marie was Polly Perkins, who married Crusoe (the plot was not entirely Defoe's). And there were Dan Leno, Herbert Campbell and Little Tich. *The Times* gave Leno the kindest review: 'from beginning to end the funniest person on the stage'; but with Little Tich it was distinctly unpleasant, describing him as 'considerably less repulsive ... than the average dwarf'.

Before *Robinson Crusoe* completed its run, Little Tich contrived to land both himself and Marie in trouble. It was an incident which shows how much humour has changed in the last century. In one scene, Marie had to kneel by her bedside and say her prayers. One night, Little Tich, who was standing in the wings, thought he would replace the sentimental with the hilarious. He shouted at Marie: 'Look under the bed'. She did, and then, not finding what she was expecting, proceeded to search the stage. A joke about a chamber pot! The audience was reduced to hysterics. The company thought it was funny, too. But Harris was furious. He felt Marie had breached the rules of decency and he seriously considered sacking her. He relented, but it was the last time either Marie or Little Tich appeared at Drury Lane.

## Chapter 8

## 1894

# DIVORCE PROCEEDINGS AND A RETURN TO AMERICA

*Robinson Crusoe* was as spectacular as any of Harris's pantomimes. Its high point was another procession – this time representing the kings and queens of England from William the Conqueror to Queen Victoria. But it was his biggest failure: he lost about £30,000 on the show. Its musical director, Jimmy Glover, blamed the injection of too much music-hall into pantomime: 'Ada Blanche excepted, each of [the] artistes introduced songs totally foreign to the story, its sentiment and its character and thoroughly unsuited to children.' (Glover 1911)

The immense amount of work and responsibility Harris took upon himself started to affect his health. He missed the opening night – the only time he did so during his entire reign at Drury Lane. In fact, Harris was so ill he was confined to his bed for eight weeks of the run.

It was an unhappy time for Marie, too. Her marriage was over; she could no longer put up with Courtenay's cruelty. They decided to live apart – Marie in Tufnell Park, Courtenay in Lewisham. Before many weeks had passed, Courtenay again proved how cruel he could be. During the season of London halls which immediately followed *Robinson Crusoe*, he turned up one night at the stage door of the Empire as Marie was about to leave for another theatre. With a hooked stick in his hand, he threatened her: ' "You are not going into that brougham tonight. I will gouge your eyes out and ruin you." ' (*Era* 23 June 1894)

Marie ran back into the theatre and stayed there for about ten minutes while Courtenay swore at her from outside. Eventually, she made a dash for the brougham with some women friends. As they left, Courtenay pushed his stick through the window of the brougham, hurting Bella Orchard. At midnight that night, he appeared at the

52

Princes Tavern in Wardour Street, a pub Marie had bought for her parents, and again threatened her: ' "I am going to —————— well murder you tonight. I will shoot you stone dead and you will never go on the stage any more." ' (*Era* 23 June 1894)

Courtenay was charged with 'having used threats to his wife, whereby she apprehended that she went in danger of her life or of some bodily harm being done to her'. (*Era* 16 June 1894) He appeared at Marlborough Street Police Court. In mitigation, his solicitor said he had gone to the Empire to remonstrate with Marie over 'certain persons' (*Era* 16 June 1894) he intended to name as co-respondents in a divorce action against her. Given his previous record, he emerged from court a lucky man. He was again ordered to keep the peace for six months, with the alternative of a month in prison.

Early in the year, there was the first hint of a development that would threaten the well-being of music-hall. Between the turns at the Empire, there was an exhibition of moving pictures – the first ever shown in Britain; but it was not very impressive, and no one thought it would catch on.

During the London season, spanning March, April and May, Marie played, in addition to the Empire, the Oxford,[4] the South London, the Metropolitan, the Middlesex, the Paragon and Sadlers Wells, which became a music-hall when George Belmont took it over in 1893. Well-known for his tongue-twisting alliterations, he called Marie a 'breathing bud of beautifulness'; 'marvellous Merrie Marie', and, on one occasion, 'tasty, trippy, twiggy, timely, telling, tender, tempting, toothsome, transcendent, trim, tactical, twinkling, tricksy, triumphal and tantalising'! (Gallagher 1971)

During June and early July, she appeared at the Star, Dublin; the Empire, Swansea; the Empire, Newport; the Empire, Cardiff, and the Tivoli, Leicester. She had one week back at London halls before making appearances at the Alhambra, Brighton; Derby Castle, Douglas, Isle of Man, and the Gaiety Palace of Varieties, Birmingham. Of the 1894 clutch of songs, Joe Tabrar had written 'A Bird In The Hand' for her:

> I once heard my dear mother say
> 'Twas wicked to be poor
> And that possession was at least
> A good nine points in law
> So, as the first young man I had
> Endeavoured to deceive
> I exercised the practice
> Which I'd been taught to believe
> A bird in the hand's worth two in the bush any time

A bird in the hand's worth two in the bush any time
He bought me a diamond ring
Well, you can understand
He had the bird in the bush
And I had the ring on my hand.

There was also 'The Spanish Senora', written by E.W. Rogers:

The Spanish senora, the swells all adore her
And often before her guitars they will strum
She trips on her toe a bit
Her ankles to show a bit
Don't you think she doesn't know a bit
Tiddle-um-pom-pom!

With Marie's parents now running her pub, it was appropriate that another of her new songs was 'The Barmaid', also written by E.W. Rogers:

The Barmaid, the Barmaid, the idol of the Rose and Crown
Since she's been there with chat and cheek
She's raised the trade a hundred a week.
The saucy swells, the horsey swells
Were never known to drink so
For she's so gay, the men all say
Awf'lly jolly girl, don't you think so?
Tol-loll, then Poll, until tonight!
The Empire? See you there? All right.
I never knew a lady wink so.
Awf'lly jolly girl, don't you think so?

[In slang, a gay woman was a prostitute.]

It was an open secret that prostitutes used the promenade which ran behind the Circle at the Empire in London. Rent-boys, too, used both the Empire and the Alhambra. It was at these two halls that Oscar Wilde's friend Alfred Taylor found some of the young men who eventually brought about Wilde's downfall. But the male prostitutes were not as obvious as their female counterparts. The women did their best to emulate fashionable courtesans. Marie's biographer, Walter MacQueen-Pope, was only one who took a romantic view of them.

These women were astounding in their professional magnificence. With the slow but dignified gait of caged tigresses, they promenaded up and down or sat at tables to be entertained by men. They drank with you, they laughed and talked with you, but they seldom accosted you and never importuned ... some of them married men they met at the Empire and, astounding as it may seem, made good wives and mothers. (MacQueen-Pope 1947)

But Mrs Ormiston Chant saw them differently. Opposing the renewal of the Empire's licence at a meeting of the County Council, she said:

> I want the amusements of London conducted in such a manner that young men and women will be able to meet together for social happiness without fear of being confronted with libertines and the keepers of questionable houses ... Lead us not into temptation, but do away with the foul spots where temptation exists. Sweep them away and London shall be happier and England better, free from the horrid slavery so many poor women are bound to. (Chant 1895)

George Edwardes, the urbane manager of the Empire, argued that, if the theatre were closed, 700 people would be thrown out of work. But the Council sided with Mrs Ormiston Chant, and the Empire was closed on 27 October.

One young man was incensed. Winston Churchill, then a cadet at Sandhurst, wrote to his father, Lord Randolph Churchill:

> The Empire is closed. The last scene was quite pathetic. On Friday night, the whole audience remained after the fall of the curtain, groaning the County Council [sic] and calling for George Edwardes, who eventually came forward and made a short speech, when a scene of extraordinary enthusiasm took place – the great audience standing up and cheering themselves hoarse. But Saturday, the place was closed and the prudes have gained a great victory. (Churchill 1966)

On 2 November, the Empire reopened with canvas screens placed between the promenade and the auditorium. The following night, Churchill was in the audience, together with a number of university graduates and other young men from Sandhurst. All agreed with each other that they did not like the look of the screens. Churchill wrote:

> Suddenly, a most strange thing happened. The entire crowd, numbering some two or three hundred people, became excited and infuriated. They rushed upon these flimsy barricades and tore them to pieces. The authorities were powerless ... In these somewhat unvirginal surroundings, I now made my maiden speech. Mounting on the debris and indeed partially emerging from it, I addressed the tumultuous crowd ... I ... appealed directly to sentiment and even passion, finishing up by saying 'You have seen us tear down these barricades tonight. See that you pull down those who are responsible for them at the coming election.' (Churchill 1930)

It was eventually ruled that the Council had exceeded its powers. The promenade stayed. On Firework Night, there were many effigies of Mrs Chant and Mr McDougall burnt on bonfires. Shaw, who had an opinion about everything, challenged Mrs Chant and an equally vociferous member of the National Vigilance Association, Lady Isabella Somerset,[5] to produce a workable definition of 'impurity'. In a letter to the *Pall Mall Gazette*, he wanted to know whether it was the possession of a sexual function; a desire to exercise that function; the clothing of the body in a particular way; all sexual intercourse; selling sexual intercourse; desiring the renewal of the Empire and Palace Theatre licences, or any one of a number of other tongue-in-cheek definitions.

To Marie, the Empire probably represented not so much the haunt of prostitutes as the place where her husband had threatened to kill her. Divorce proceedings began, with Courtenay alleging that Marie had committed adultery with two men – one at her home in Tufnell Park and the other on a houseboat she had taken on the Thames at Datchet in Buckinghamshire.

With the threat of all this hanging over her, Marie left Liverpool for her second visit to America. She was to appear for six weeks at the Imperial Theatre in New York at a salary of £100 a week. While she was away, Courtenay dropped the divorce proceedings. But Marie sailed from one set of legal complexities to another. On her first trip to America, she had had some of her thunder stolen by another entertainer. On her second, there were complications over her contract. The contract she had signed stipulated that she must obey the rules of the theatre, but it neglected to say what the rules were. Marie complained to the Press:

> Mr Kraus [the manager of the Imperial] has been making new rules whenever he feels like it. He has done everything to annoy and humiliate me and all because he wanted to back out of his contract and save 500 dollars a week by so doing. Why, after I had been entering his place by the front door for three weeks, he told me I would have to go down the area stairs to the stage door – the rat pit, I call it – and once I did that. Then, he made another order that I should have to report at the music-hall at eight, although I did not go on till 10.30. Then, when I sat in the house or in the café, waiting until it was time to make up, he told me everyone was required to stay in the dressing-rooms and he had a lot of cages full of trained dogs and monkeys stuck up in front of my door until the place smelt like a menagerie. Sunday night he had the effrontery to tell me I was drunk and he used a great deal of vulgar and insulting language to me then. He tried to prevent my doctor from coming to see me and had the doorkeeper threaten to call a policeman to arrest him. Yesterday, I got a letter telling me to report for a

rehearsal this morning prepared with new songs. I have already sung eighteen different songs in the four weeks I have been here – and I don't propose to sing any more new ones till I want to and so I told Mr Kraus. Today, I get a notice that my contract was broken. (*Entr'acte* 27 October 1894)

Unfortunately, that was not the end of Marie's problems. Two years previously, she had signed a contract with Koster and Bial, for whom she had worked in 1890. The contract included a $1,000 forfeit clause, and, since Marie had broken it, Koster and Bial began litigation to try to obtain the money due to her from the Imperial. That problem, at least, was solved by Marie appearing for Koster and Bial during the last fortnight of her visit.[6]

Marie drew good audiences on her second visit to America. But the problems at the Imperial had made it an unpleasant time, not rendered any easier by her voyage home being abnormally rough. Still, she returned to the Oxford, the Middlesex and the Cambridge, according to one reviewer, in the best of voice and ready to face a new challenge – pantomime in Liverpool.

# Chapter 9

## 1895

# MARIE'S HELPING HAND

For just over two months, Marie was Boy Blue in *Pretty Bo-Peep* at the Shakespeare theatre. The *Stage* praised her: 'Miss Marie Lloyd is an established source of joy and amusement and the delicious naivete and delightful piquancy of this clever lady are visible in all she does.'

The highlight of the show was a parody of a well-known Gus Elen song, ' 'E Dunno Where 'E Are'. Marie's version was 'There Goes the Bloke who Dunno Where 'E Are'; and she paid public thanks to the man who wrote it for her – Alec Hurley, a coster singer who was beginning to make himself known.

In March, Marie was back in London, playing four halls a night – the Pavilion, the Middlesex, the Tivoli and the Canterbury. At about this time, she met a young mimic, Ronnie Hutchinson, who had begun his professional life working for the sugar refining firm of Henry Tate. Marie was impressed by his act. 'Change your name' she told him, 'and I'll get you an audition at the Oxford.' (Gallagher 1971)

Shortly afterwards, she left for another provincial tour:

|        |                                    |
|--------|------------------------------------|
| April: | Gaiety, Birmingham                 |
|        | Empire, Newcastle                  |
| May:   | Scotia, Glasgow                    |
|        | People's Palace, Bradford          |
|        | Alhambra, Brighton                 |
|        | Thornton's Varieties, South Shields |
| June:  | Princess Palace, Leeds             |

By now, Marie was earning good money in the provinces. For her week in Bradford, she was paid £100. That was such a startling amount of money that, once the cheque had been cashed, it was framed and hung up in the theatre's bar. While Marie was away Ronnie Hutchinson took her advice. Modifying his employer's name, he became Harry Tate. He was given six weeks' work at the Oxford at a wage of £4 a week. Soon, his impersonations of, among others, Dan Leno and the eccentric comic T.E. Dunville, earned him an enthusiastic following. Within a few years, Harry Tate was one of the leading comics of his generation.

Although successful, Harry Tate was not the number one topic among theatre people towards the end of May 1895. That distinction fell to the most successful playwright of the day, Oscar Wilde. Convicted of indecency with some of the Empire and Alhambra rent-boys, he was sentenced to two years' imprisonment with hard labour. During the ordeal of two trials he faced, he was abandoned by many previous close friends. When he stood the chance of being released on bail, few of them made any effort to find the money. One of the two men who eventually stood bail had never, in fact, met Wilde. He was the Church of England's far-sighted friend of music-hall, a man who knew what disgrace felt like – Stewart Headlam.

Besides Wilde, there was another big literary talking-point that year – *Trilby*, a novel by the French writer George du Maurier, originally published in parts in *Harper's Magazine*. One of its main characters, the Trilby of the title, was a model who wore the style of hat that from that date bore her name. The other main character was a musician, Svengali, under whose spell she fell. The plot caused a craze that swept Britain and the United States. There were Trilby parties, Trilby shoes, even Trilby sweets. Eventually, the book was made into a play with the role of Svengali taken by Wilde's friend, Beerbohm Tree, the half-brother of Max Beerbohm. Marie also wanted to exploit the craze, and once again, Harrington and le Brunn came up trumps with 'Tricky Little Trilby':

I'm a modern actress and I play
All the up-to-datey parts today
Serious or gay, not one is missed
Trilby is the latest on my list.
Twasn't in my line I thought because
I had no idea who Trilby was
But the pay, of course, cured my disgust
So I thought I'd play the part or bust.
They said Trilby modest ought to be,
Modest Trilby, what a part for me
Quiet and prim, me? No, jolly fear!
So I made Trilby quite a new idea

Trilby, Trilby, tricky and trim,
Lissom of limb, plenty of vim,
Not afraid of any young 'him'
That's the sort of Trilby

Trilby likes her bottle of fizz
Fellows to quiz, jolly good biz.
Tricky little Trilby, witty little Trilby
That's the sort of Trilby this girl is.

In the third verse, Harrington had some fun at his collaborator's expense:

When we reached the mesmerising part
When I find my voice and lose my heart.
Where the music man does this for fun
Something in the style of George le Brunn ...

During the London season that followed the provincial tour, Marie was on the same bill at the Oxford with Alec Hurley, the man who had helped to make her Liverpool pantomime such a success. That autumn, she had a collection of new songs to try out – besides 'Tricky Little Trilby', there were 'Near Thing', 'The Rich Girl and the Poor Girl', 'Salute my Bicycle' and another George le Brunn/W.T. Lytton composition, 'What's That For, Eh?' (also known as 'Johnny Jones and I Know Now'):

I don't like boys, they are so rude
I would not like them if I could
Well, Johnny Jones, he's not so low
He tells me things what I don't know
One day, a rude boy pulled my hair
And, though I cried, he didn't care
He only laughed and went like so
[There was some movement or gesticulation here]
So off I ran to Ma to know
What's that for, eh? Oh! Tell me, Ma
If you don't tell me, I'll ask Pa
But Ma said 'Oh it's nothing, shut your row'
Well, I've asked Johnny Jones, see! So, I know now.

During the autumn, Marie played five halls – the Tivoli, the Pavilion, Sadlers Wells, the Varieties, Hoxton, and the Queens, Poplar. By now, she was quite used to adapting her act from one hall to another. The routine fascinated a journalist from the *Sketch*, who accompanied her one night in her brougham, recording how she was received by each audience. In Hoxton and Poplar, she sang 'Near Thing', 'The Rich Girl and the Poor Girl' and 'Salute My Bicycle'. At both halls, it was the second song that went down best. At the stage door of the Varieties, she was presented with a huge cut-glass bottle of scent by a group of East End girls. On the way to Sadlers Wells, another group of girls threw a large box of expensive sweets into the brougham. At Sadlers Wells, Marie kept the 'Bicycle Song' in her act, but replaced the other two with 'Trilby' and 'What's That For, Eh?'. The *Sketch* man noted that the Sadlers Wells audience were mystified by 'Trilby': 'Though, as a song, it went well, few of the audience, I ween, knew much of the lady ... I had various enquiries among the audience as to who Trilby was ... The Bicycle song, on the other hand, was thoroughly understood and appreciated, as was another innovation entitled What's That For?'

At the Tivoli and the Pavilion, the *Sketch* reporter found the reception much different. 'How thoroughly they understood and appreciated every line of Trilby O'Ferrall up to date, the Cyclist [Salute My Bicycle] and the Baby song [What's That For?]; but though the applause at both these places for Marie Lloyd's songs was magnificent, it was no warmer and certainly not so uproarious as that in the East-End halls.' He attributed that to the fact that everyone in the 'gods' knew something of Marie's astonishing philanthropy. At that time, she was paying each night for 150 beds for the homeless and destitute of the East End. It was a generosity she maintained for the rest of her days. At every turn, she helped her family as well as her music-hall colleagues – not just professionally, but materially. And she helped countless others who were unknown to her. The comedian Arthur Roberts wrote:

> As she was in her youth, so she was to the day of her death, the most improvidently generous woman whom I have ever met. Throughout her life, she had an open heart and I cannot think of anybody who ever went to her with an open hand who did not leave the stage door with something to put in his pocket. She used to ask me to wait for her after her show to protect her from the sharks who were always hanging about the wings ready to seize hold of all her earnings. (Roberts 1927)

Marie's kindness to others was demonstrated in a variety of ways. To some, like Harry Tate, she gave professional help. When Georgie Wood was beginning his career, he included impersonations in his act, among which was one of Marie. When the two of them were appearing at different theatres in Glasgow, Marie asked to see him. He feared he was going to be reprimanded. Instead, Marie offered to help him improve the impersonation, teaching him all the movements and intonations of one of her songs. Georgie said later: 'No-one could – and very few would – have taken such trouble over helping a young artiste.' (Ross unpublished)

Marie helped the young Hetty King in another way. Hetty, who was appearing at the Oxford, shared a dressing-room with a number of older women, including Marie and a sharp-tongued chaperone her father had employed. One night, the chaperone took her to task for not doing precisely what she should have done in one of her songs. She gave Hetty a sharp cuff round the ears, adding 'If you do that again tomorrow night, I'll give you the biggest thrashing you've ever had.' At that, Marie intervened: 'I warn you, my lady, that, if you lay a finger on that little girl, I'll let you know all about it'; and then, turning to a frightened Hetty: 'As for you, my love, stop crying. No one will harm you. I'll see to that.' (Ross unpublished)

# Chapter 10

## 1896

# *THE BLUE BOOK AND THE PURITANS*

Tragedy struck Marie at the turn of the year with the death of her agent, George Ware. Throughout the profession he was greatly respected, more than living up to his nickname of the Old Reliable. He came from the same background as Marie, and had been born in Shoreditch in 1829. At the outset of his career, he appeared on the halls in a comedy act with his wife. He was also a prolific song-writer. His greatest pride, though, was the discovery of Marie. He alone could claim the credit of making a star of her while she was still in her teens.

Gus Harris, too, was to leave Marie's life, as workaholism finally caught up with him. Mrs Clement Scott, the wife of the *Daily Telegraph*'s drama critic, recalled how hard Harris would drive himself (and everyone else) at rehearsals: 'He'd put the whole crowd through its paces, shouting and raving at them all the while like a lunatic. He simply insisted on everything being done *his* way. I have known him stick for nineteen hours at a stretch until certain scenes in a play were as he intended them to be.' (Clement Scott 1918) Gus Harris died at the age of 44. Marie grieved briefly for both men.

Then, it was straight back to work. Early in 1896, she was at the London Pavilion, the Oxford, the Tivoli and the South London with a number of new songs – among them, 'Chance Your Luck', on which George le Brunn had collaborated with Wal Pink.

> When you roll home rather late
> Which is not the proper form for you,
> And you know, as on you roam, that for coming so late home,
> Your wife will make things warm for you,
> Standing on the bottom stair
> Is a female figure there
> Well, you've no chance of missing her

THE NEXT NEW AUTHORESS.

MISS MARIE LLOYD.

Marie wrote a little book, which she described as "Blue:"
The public bought it chiefly for its cerulean hue.

As you open the street door
If you're not a fool, I'm sure
To square her, you'll start kissing her.

Chance your luck, chance your luck
You kiss her quick, then find out by and bye
That the one who got the kisses
Is the slavey, not the missis
Well, you never know your luck until you try.

There were five verses, in all, with the same advice in each chorus.
The second verse dealt with trying to pick up a girl, who was used to
having money spent on her:

Say 'I can't afford you silks, you can have a plate of whelks'
For you never know your luck until you try.

Another 1896 song was just as successful – 'Among My
Knick-Knacks', which George le Brunn wrote with W.T. Lytton.

I am a giddy tourist and photography's my game
Always on the job with my camera
Quite devoted to my art, I can give most folks a start
I'm A-1 at Lloyds with the camera
I sometimes entertain my friends with views I have in stock
But oft some cruel defect in a picture I detect
For instance in this lovely view I took of London Docks
I find a fat old girl engaged in pulling up her socks.

There you are! Picture spoilt!
Not fit to place among my bric-bracs
Every picture that I find of a rather tasty kind
I put it in my drawer among my knick-knacks.

The last verse made a topical reference to the invention of X–rays
the previous year:

No doubt, you all have heard about the New Photography
Wonders we can work with the camera
Photograph you through and through is the latest thing we do
So, mind how you go with the camera
By this most startling plan our very bones are brought to view
And stranger still to tell, the brain and thoughts as well
One evening at the ballet I was sitting just behind
A Johnny and I took the chance to photograph his mind

'Pon my word! Picture great!
But not fit to place among my bric-bracs
Oh the pretty thoughts he thunk
Well, they'd petrify a monk
So I keep it in my drawer among my knick-knacks.

Marie played halls in London until the end of May, when she set off on her longest provincial tour to date. For some reason, little effort was given to ensuring she had as short a distance as possible to travel between the last house on the Saturday night and the band call in a new town on the following Monday. It was nothing to be in Lancashire one week and Kent the next, or to travel on a Sunday from one hard week in Newcastle to another in Brighton:

| | |
|---|---|
| June: | Empire, Blackpool |
| | Gaiety, Chatham |
| | Empire, Leicester |
| | Princess Palace, Leeds |
| July: | Scotia, Glasgow |
| | Empire, Birmingham |
| | Empire, Newcastle |
| | Alhambra, Brighton |
| August: | Town Hall, Folkestone |
| | Kiernan's, Liverpool |
| | Pavilion, Douglas |
| September | Empire, Blackpool |

During the summer, there was some publicity about an autobiography of Marie, which was apparently being ghosted by a writer called Frank Rogers. The title it was given – *Marie Lloyd's Blue Book* – was a play on words. Blue books were government publications; but everyone knew what Marie meant by 'blue'. The pun helped to underline her growing reputation for being *risquée*.

The music-hall press made rather prim references to the book. The *Encore* reported: 'The title of the book is a colour that will make it read:' while the *Entr'acte* carried a full-page cartoon entitled 'The Next New Authoress' together with a rhyme: 'Marie wrote a little book, which she described as "Blue"; The public bought it chiefly for its cerulean hue.'

The question is: did the public buy it? Or rather: was it ever published? The *Era* printed a review, which said it contained 'a number of Marie's axioms, many American stories and ... a comedy in one act ...' It also quoted from the book, apparently verbatim, concentrating on a number of proposals of marriage which it is said

Marie had had. One of them, probably apochryphal, gave Marie the chance to retaliate against the puritans. An admirer had written:

> Dear Sister, Having been induced to go to an unholy place of entertainment, I saw you for the first time last Monday and I have been three times since. I am sure you need a life-long consolation of unity with one who treads in the path of righteousness. I am a temperance orator and, never having tasted alcoholic beverages, I would make a good partner for life. If you will wed me, I will not object to you still earning your wages in an unrighteous music-hall. (*Era* 1 August 1896)

In reply, Marie said she told him that he was no use to her, as she believed that: 'The man who warms himself on a cold night with a large glass of whisky would make a better husband than the one who went to bed shivering and digging his cold knees in his wife's back.' (*Era* 1 August 1896)

If the *Blue Book* ever reached the shops, few copies survived. No major library has one and the main specialist dealers have never seen it.

Marie's crop of songs in 1896 were particularly saucy. One was 'Maid of London, Ere We Part', a parody on 'The Maid of Athens', a ballad that used Byron's words:

> Maid of Athens! ere we part, ere we part,
> Give, oh give me back my heart
> Or since that has left my breast,
> Keep it now and take the rest. (Byron 1886)

'Maid of London' was the work of Harrington, le Brunn and Joseph Tabrar:

> Maid of London, ere we part, ere we part,
> Give, oh give me back my heart, back my heart
> Since though hast gone from my breast, from my breast,
> Keep the stick with a silver knob
> Given me by a certain snob
> Give me back my thingamy bob
> And you can keep the rest

Together with another song, 'Johnny Jones', it ensured that Marie was given a particularly rough ride when London County Council's Theatres and Music-Halls Committee met in October to decide which halls should be licensed for the following year. Objections were again lodged to the use of theatre promenades by prostitutes; and a number of songs, including three of Marie's came in for criticism.

Carina Reed, representing the Social Purity Branch of the British Women's Temperance Association, opposed the renewal of the Oxford's licence because she did not like the third and fourth verses of 'Johnny Jones':

Pa took me up to town one day,
To see the shops and sights so gay
Oh how the ladies made me stare
They nearly all had yellow hair
And one of them – oh, what a shame!
She called Pa 'Bertie' – it's not his name
Then went like *this* and winked her eye
And so I said to Pa 'Oh my!'
  What's that for, eh? (etc)

Ah, I know something no one knows
Ma's making oh such pretty clothes
Too large for dolly they must be
I'm sure they're much too small for me
There's little frocks and socks and shoes
And ribbons – reds and pinks and blues
And little bibs as well there are
And other things, so I asked Ma
  What's that for, eh? (etc).

An academic analysis of a music-hall lyric has as little impact as the explanation of a joke. Miss Reed made herself look ludicrous by suggesting that the references to the mother's work in the fourth verse were indecent. Under cross-examination, the Oxford's manager, Harry Lundy, said he did not see that a girl with yellow hair need be bad. As for baby clothes, said Lundy, they might be made for anyone.

The Pavilion's licence was opposed on account of 'Johnny Jones' and another song 'That Was a Bloomer'. The objectors admitted they were upholding the cause initiated by Mrs Chant. But even she had lost some of her influence since the furore about the Empire's promenade two years previously. Throughout the music-hall profession, she was no more than a laughing-stock. One joke was told by the quickfire American comedian, R.G. Knowles: 'Mrs Chant went to heaven. She knocked at the door. "Who's there?" asked St Peter. "Mrs Chant" was the reply. So, Peter put the catch on the door and shouted "Angels! Put on your pyjamas!" ' (Greenwall 1936)

At one stage during the committee's proceedings, Councillor H.H. Marks said he and his colleagues had no wish to set a standard of songs for music-halls, but they did want to eliminate 'lines or patter, which [were] obviously of an improper nature'. (*The Globe* 15 October 1896)

The Oxford and Pavilion were granted their licences, but there was a rider from the committee – that 'greater care ought to be exercised in the selection of songs'. (*The Globe* 15 October 1896) As a result, the management of the Pavilion ordered all artistes to submit their songs three days in advance. And so, the committee had succeeded in cleaning up the halls by persuading managers to do it for them.

Marie's way of retaliating against the puritans was to ask Harrington, le Brunn and Tabrar to write a song that left everything to the audience's imagination – 'You Can't Stop A Girl From Thinking':

> I mustn't tell you what I mean
> Mustn't tell you what I've seen
> Everything that's risky must be dropped
> Well, I've been stopped for winking
> Mustn't tell you what I've heard
> Mustn't say a naughty word
> So help my bob, it's a jolly good job
> They can't stop a girl from thinking.

During the autumn, Marie appeared in a number of London halls with the exception of a fortnight in December, when she starred at the Regent Theatre, Salford, followed by the Gaiety, Chatham. She also announced that, early in 1897, she meant to win a new audience. She was to visit South Africa for the first time to appear at the Empire, Johannesburg. Unfortunately, as with her first visit to New York, she suffered from another entertainer singing her songs before she arrived. This time, she got the Empire's proprietor, Edgar Hyman, to stop it. In advertisements she placed in the music-hall press to thank him, she added: 'Have been asked especially to sing my famous Johnny Jones to let the public see the way it should be sung, not murdered. Look out! I have some stunners up my sleeve.' (*Era* 14 November 1896)

# Chapter 11

## 1897

# SOUTH AFRICA, AMERICA AND HOME AGAIN

Marie's send-off from Britain was as warm as her reception in South Africa. The Sunday before she left, 160 of her friends had dinner at the Trocadero Restaurant in Piccadilly to say goodbye. Afterwards, everyone danced until 3.30 a.m. On the morning of the voyage, another huge crowd thronged Waterloo Station to see her off and weigh her down with flowers and presents. At Southampton, railway staff filled the platform, as though awaiting a royal train. Many more people lined the quayside at the docks, which were festooned with Union Jacks. Marie was handed a huge parcel of telegrams, wishing her a safe journey and good luck in Johannesburg. There was only one sour note. Courtenay – in a belated show of interest in his young daughter – tried to prevent her joining her mother. But the child was smuggled aboard the liner at the last moment to join her mother, her aunt Rosie and Bella Orchard. Marie finally gave way to the emotion of the occasion and burst into tears. As the liner pulled away from the quayside, she stood on deck, bidding everyone goodbye. Her waving handkerchief could be seen until the ship was almost out of sight.

Marie's six-week engagement at the Johannesburg Empire was so successful that Edgar Hyman extended it to eight. Inevitably, her audience had heard that she might be rude. But the critics found otherwise: 'There is no tinge of anything in the least objectionable in Miss Marie's repertoire and the rumours to the contrary have been wildly exaggerated.' (*The Transvaal Critic*); 'Her quips, cranks and merry conceits are of the Pink 'Un genre, it is true, but they are wrapped up with the skill of an artiste and the naughty is not too naughtily apparent.' (*Standard and Diggers News*, the authorised government gazette for Witwatersrand).

MR. DAN LENO, TO MISS MARIE LLOYD:— "WELL, I WISH YOU A BIG SUCCESS
AND A SPEEDY RETURN, MARIE!"—AND SO SAY ALL OF US.

During the trip, Marie entertained as lavishly as ever. The small bungalow in which she stayed became a centre for some of South Africa's diamond millionaires – among them one of the country's wealthiest men, Barney Barnato. One afternoon, Marie junior started mimicking Barnato, much to his amusement. He told Hyman about the girl's talent and, in no time at all, she was appearing at the Empire herself. Her fee for two weeks' work was £100 – money she never saw, for her mother pocketed it. For years afterwards, that was a family joke. If Marie refused Marie junior a loan, the rejoinder was usually: 'What about the £100 I earned in Africa?'

Marie was by now a star in three continents – a well-travelled young woman. One of her new songs in 1897 was about a young woman rather less worldly-wise – 'What Did She Know About the Railways', written by Bennett Scott and C.G. Cotes:

> She arrived at Euston by the midnight train
> But, when she got to the wicket
> There someone wanted to punch her ticket
> The guards and porters came round her by the score
> And she told them all she'd never had a ticket punched before.

The song showed, if proof were needed, that a *double entendre* can be read into practically anything. In the summer of 1897, Marie ran into another censorship row, though not with that song, but with another called '(Won't You Be My) Saturday to Monday'. She wanted to sing it at the London Pavilion, but she refused to submit the lyrics to the management in advance. The row came to a head when the theatre's directors took a box to see if she was going to obey their instructions. She did not and, as a result, she was told her contract would be cancelled. The *Encore* felt a scapegoat was being made of her. In its view, George Robey and T.E. Dunville sang songs that were equally suggestive. Nonetheless, Marie was off the Pavilion bill for a few weeks, though the dispute was eventually settled and she was allowed back. Among Marie's admirers, the theatre critic James Agate saw no vulgarity:

> Would-be apologists have pleaded that 'whilst many of the songs were in themselves offensive, the manner of their delivery took away the offence.' This is the purest nonsense. The genius of this diseuse consisted in the skill and emphasis with which she drove home the 'offensive' point. She emphasised a whole armoury of shrugs and leers and to reveal every cranny of the mind utilised each articulation of the body. (Agate 1945)

That summer, in addition to halls in London, Marie also played the Empire, Newcastle; the Empire, Swansea, and the Empire, Cardiff. But she now had the travel bug. In August, she set off for Germany to appear at the Winter Gardens in Berlin for a month.

Another of Marie's new songs in 1897 was about a foreigner struggling to find the right words – 'Vat Ze English Call Ze', written by Le Brunn and Mon Tresor. This is the second verse and chorus:

One evening, he informed me in his own peculiar style
He'd been to take the air up Piccadilly way;
To tell it as he told it would engage me such a while
And perhaps you'd think it too a very silly way.
Said he 'Sweet madame, zere I met
In conver-za-ze-ong ve did get
She said 'No husband I have got
But children, she possess a lot.' She vas –

Vat ze English ze – vat ze name?
On my tongue I have ze very word to fit
Vat smile so sweet at me (*pause*)
I have it! – ha – oui, oui –
Ze widow – zat vas it.

On September 21, Marie left Bremen for Southampton, and on the following day she sailed on to America – her third visit there. She was back at Koster and Bial's.[7]

Marie had half-a-dozen songs that were new to Koster and Bial's clientele – among them 'Saturday to Monday'. It caused no fuss in New York. By and large, she attracted laudatory notices. (One reviewer noted she was plumper than she had been in 1894.) The *New York Herald* critic wrote this: 'The songs wouldn't exactly "go" in a church fair in Four Corners, Vermont, and the audience at some Broadway theatres might not relish them, but they were not, apparently, too tabasco-like in their flavour for a music-hall audience.'

As always, there was something to spoil the trip. This time it centred on one bad review. Back in England, Marie took an advertisement in *Entr'acte*: 'Many thanks to the kind creature, who took the trouble to send a copy of a two-cent print with an adverse criticism of myself to all the proprietors in London ... What a dreadful complaint, jealousy.'

On Boxing Day, Marie had a new audience to conquer. She had never previously appeared at the Palace Theatre in Cambridge Circus. It had been thought that Marie would not appeal to the fashionable, after-dinner crowd the theatre attracted. In any case – said the critics – if she did appear at the Palace, she would have to tone her act down.

Marie did nothing of the sort. She sang with her usual audacity and the audience, which included the Queen's cousin, the Duke of Cambridge, applauded her twice as much as anyone else on the bill.

# Chapter 12

## 1898–99

# THE FILM, THE PHONOGRAPH AND *DICK WHITTINGTON*

In 1898, Marie embarked on her one and only venture into musical comedy. She took the title role in *The ABC Girl*, playing Flossie the Frivolous, a waitress in one of the Aerated Bread Company's cafés. Some of the show's music was by Graban, a *nom de plume* for a more serious musician, Granville Bantock, professor of music at Birmingham University. The director was his brother, Leedham, who had appeared in many of George Edwardes' shows, including *A Gaiety Girl* and *The Shop Girl*. The Bantocks collaborated with H. Chance Newton, who was given the job of writing the book only a fortnight before curtain up. When the idea was put to him, his first inclination was to turn it down: 'What! Are you dotty? ... Why, Marie's starting date is a fortnight's hence. You must find something ready made. No new play can be written, rehearsed and produced in such a time for such a star!' (Newton 1928) But he was persuaded: 'I wrote that play for Marie, scene by scene and song by song, at a series of day and night rehearsals, with the composers, scene setters, dress designers, chorus etc. by my side, and engaging people as I went along.' (op.cit.)

The show toured for eight weeks, starting in Wolverhampton, then travelling to Dublin, Nottingham, Sheffield and Stratford East. Although the backers announced that it would return in the autumn, it was, in fact, quietly laid to rest. Kurt Ganzl explained the reason for its short life:

Although it was tailored well to its purpose, that purpose was not a particularly valid one. Miss Lloyd could shine more brightly and more freely in the halls in her own most attractive character – there was no need for her to assume another – and her devotees were frankly more

75

interested in seeing Marie than in seeing Flossie, no matter how frivolous. (Ganzl and Lamb 1988)

Although her career was as successful as ever, Marie was wise to keep an eye on new developments in popular theatre. Besides musical comedy, film was now a regular feature of music-hall bills, just two years after making its début. By the summer of 1898, a 30– to 40–minute film show was part of the programme in more than a hundred halls up and down the country. In addition, more and more entertainers were recording cylinders. The *Encore* pointed out what it saw as the dangers:

> Imagine, for example, a great Variety Artiste, like Arthur Roberts or Dan Leno, displayed on film in the act of singing a song, while Edison's latest improved Phonograph is grinding out the song with as clear an intonation as the singers themselves could give, if they were actually on the stage. A provincial Music Hall man pays a sovereign a night for a film of five or six songs or dances and the live Artiste, who has to eat, drink and live, is displaced by the reflection, which requires none of these things. Of course, it would be very excellent business for the Lenos and the Campbells, the Marie Lloyds and the Lottie Collinses, but, for the struggling artiste, it would spell trouble of a very sinister kind. Yet, it is going to come and the thin end of the wedge is the phonographic instrument, into which certain big singers have sung their songs quite thoughtlessly.

Marie had yet to commit herself to wax, although two songs she sang in 1898 would have proved very popular to the small, but growing, record-buying public. One of them – about a pair of young lovers – had a melody, which George le Brunn had adapted freely from *Narcissus*, written by an American composer, Ethelbert Nevin, in 1891. Fred Murray and Fred W. Leigh wrote the words of 'There They Are, The Two Of Them On Their Own':

> Ever since sister Mary Ann took on with Mister Green
> I had had no complaints to make – I'll tell you what I mean
> Every time he makes a call, that's nearly every day
> Both of 'em seem to look on me as being in the way.
> If I go in the parlour when the pair of 'em are there
> Oh it's a lark to see the way they both begin to glare
> Mary she looks at Mister Green and then he winks his eye
> Look at me now! they've sent me out, I'm sure they don't know why!

> There they are, the pair of 'em on their own
> In the parlour alone, alone, alone
> They've given me half-a-crown to run away and play
> Li-tiddle-dy! Hi-tiddle-dy! Hi-tiddle-dy-ay!

Marie's summer tour that year lasted three months:

| | |
|---|---|
| June: | Empire, Cardiff |
| | Empire, Swansea |
| July: | Empire, Newcastle |
| August | Alhambra, Brighton[8] |
| | Argyle, Birkenhead |
| | Palace, Southampton |
| | Tivoli, Manchester |

Her other popular 1898 song – a further collaboration by Harrington and le Brunn – gave birth to a saying that is still part of the English language, 'Everything in the Garden's Lovely':

> We see a dozy youth go out in all his extra best
> And ev'rything in the garden's lovely
> A pair of patents, pair of kids and lovely flowered vest
> And ev'rything in the garden's lovely
> But suddenly, while passing by a house that's in repair
> A painter shouts 'Take care! Look out, you chap, down there!'
> Then all at once a pot of paint comes flying thro' the air
> And ev'rything in the garden's lovely!
> Ev'rything in the garden is absolutely grand
> Ev'rything in the garden is great, you'll understand!
> Wollop! comes the painter's pot And the dandy cops the lot
> Then ev'rything in the garden's lovely.

To the anti-music-hall lobby, everything in the garden was lovelier than it had been, although its members still made themselves heard occasionally. In May, Dan Godfrey, the highly respected musical director of the Winter Gardens, Bournemouth, drew up a long list of music-hall stars he wanted to present. The town's deputy Mayor ruled him out of order, saying he did not think 'variety shows were consistent with the dignity of the Corporation'. (*Encore* 9 June 1898) In the years to come, Godfrey got his way, booking – among others – Dan Leno, George Robey, Harry Lauder, Harry Tate and Vesta Tilley. But, although she appeared just down the road at Boscombe, Marie Lloyd was never allowed into hallowed Bournemouth. The *Encore* poked fun at the town's attitude:

> Oh, Bournemouth, if you would but try
> To practise what you preach
> For those who know you best say Fie
> It's Chant without the 'h'.

Although less had been heard from Mrs Chant since the uproar at the Empire, she proved in a letter to *The Times* on 4 October 1898 she had not gone completely to earth. Was she mellowing though? Her tone seemed rather more conciliatory – at least in the way she acknowledged that music-hall was here to stay:

> The music-hall fulfils a need that has sprung out of the complicated civilisation of our big towns and cities. People who toil all day in ugly places and other sordid conditions need to have somewhere to go in the evening where brightness, colour and music can help them to forget the greyness of life for a while and where sociability and laughter keep the human instinct alive and unsoured and there is no earthly reason why the supply for the demand should come from contaminated instead of pure sources.
>
> Vice is not a necessary ingredient of a comic song, nor leering and suggestive gesture the inseparable accompaniment of a skirt dance; and here is no more reason why ruffianism should be glorified in the variety entertainment than deformity or cancer or any other disease that degrades and disfigures the body. (Chant 1895)

That autumn, Marie was (privately) in a new home – Granville Lodge, King Henry's Road, St John's Wood – and (publicly) at a selection of London halls, among them the Middlesex, Collins, and the London. At Christmas, she starred in the first of three pantomimes at the Crown Theatre, Peckham. Undoubtedly, she could have chosen a more illustrious, if not a more central theatre; but she had always believed that charity began at home, and her sister Daisy was engaged to be married to the theatre's director, Donald Munro.

The pantomime was *Dick Whittington* (or *Harlequin, the Fairy Spells and the Talkative Bells*). The music was by the music-hall composer Orlando Powell, and the show was written by Geoffrey Thorn, a pantomime stalwart, who also wrote theatre criticism for *Lloyds News*, the *Observer* and the *Daily Chronicle*.

Marie played the title role, but happily loaned her newest success, 'Everything In The Garden's Lovely', to Daisy, who took the part of Alice Fitzwarren. The *Stage* praised both sisters.

> The choice of Miss Marie Lloyd was a good one and one that this clever lady has already justified. She partakes in all the fun with zest, sings with her well-known vigour and throughout exercises the charms of Marie Lloyd over the audience ... Miss Daisy Wood ... a bright and vivacious dancer ... makes so dainty an Alice that Dick's affection is easily understood.

One of the biggest successes in the show was 'Hulloa! Hulloa! Hulloa!', written by George le Brunn and George Rollit:

A lot of things we perpetrate are very nice no doubt
Until we're, by some blunder, unexpectedly found out
For instance, take the fellow, who at ball or garden fête
Retired to the conservatory to have a tête-à-tête with Kate

For if, by chance, you enter, You hear a mild report [*kiss*]
You'll say 'I beg your pardon' (or something of that sort)
And presently you see them – Her pretty face aglow
His coat one mass of powder – Hulloa! Hulloa! Hulloa!

Marie's fans sought her out, however far off the beaten track she was appearing. Of *Dick Whittington*, the *Encore* reported: 'Her true inwardness of genius was never more demonstrated than in this production and I was not surprised at being told that patrons from far-away Highgate, now that the all-night trams are in full swing, come down to see the show.'

Another of the 1899 crop of songs made further references to Marie's 'blue' reputation – 'Of Course', written by Harrington, le Brunn and J.F. Lambe:

I wouldn't tell you anything that's wrong – of course
Still, I tell you how you ought to go along – of course
You can make your love vows hotter
When you've tied the knot and got 'er – well, of course.

And, of course, she sang nothing wrong, although this was pretty near the mark – 'Everybody Wondered How He Knew', written by George Rollit and Howard Talbot:

There are often little trifles that were better left unsaid
But are uttered in an unexpected way
Which reminds me of a funny little matter which occurred
At a fashionable ball the other day,
The host espied a silk embroidered garter on the floor
And gaily dared the owner to declare
When a jolly looking fellow said without the least concern
'Oh I know it, it belongs to Missis Dair.
Now wasn't that a silly thing to say
Oh wasn't that a silly thing to do
It came as quite a starter
When he recognised the garter
For everybody wondered how he knew.

# Chapter 13

## 1900

# THE GIRL IN KHAKI TOURS THE NORTH

During the first weeks of 1900, Marie was back in pantomime at the Crown Theatre, Peckham. There was no Daisy Wood this year; but it was still a family affair, with Alice playing the starring role of Cinderella, and Tom and Fred McNaughton as a couple of comics. The writing was in familiar hands, too. The music was again arranged and selected by Orlando Powell, whilst Geoffrey Thorn took care of everything else. The *Stage* was in no doubt about its success:

> Marie (playing Prince Heliotrope) makes the pantomime ... winning by the way enthusiastic plaudits and encores by the dozen. From the moment of her effective first entrance – on horseback and in hunting costume – right away to the very conclusion of the pantomime opening, she easily holds her audience and, though in the course of the performance, she sings song after song and wears nine different costumes, each successive one more costly and becoming than the last, the delighted audience can never have had enough.

As soon as *Cinderella* closed in the middle of February Marie and Alice took a quick trip around Birmingham, Manchester and Liverpool, taking stock – as they put it – of pantomimes that were still running. For most of March, Marie played the halls in London, with a new, topical song. The Boer War was then at its height, the early months of the year having proved decisive, with the relief of Kimberley and Ladysmith followed by that of Mafeking. Political satire was never a feature of Marie's act. But she felt there was some fun to be had at the amount of khaki suddenly to be seen on the streets. Harrington and le Brunn found the right mixture for her in 'The Girl in the Khaki Dress'.

MISS MARIE LLOYD.

"THE GIRL IN THE KHAKI DRESS."

I am a girl who's rather larky
Always dressing myself in khaki
Just the same as men who claim to fight for their home and Queen
Now, they're winning a nation's praises
You all know what the latest craze is
Khaki this and khaki that! Well, I'm on in that scene
Khaki boots and stockings on either leg
And ev'ry morn at breakfast time I have a khaki egg
Khaki cuffs and collars, yes, and khaki 'Dicky dirts'
And I've got khaki bloomers on underneath my skirts!
I'm the girl in the khaki dress
Fellows following me, so larky
Busmen holloa-ing 'Wotcha khaki'
Oh, girls, their love they can't express
What oh! That's Flo! the girl in the khaki dress!

If the reference to bloomers was near the knuckle, what can Mr McDougall and Mrs Chant have made of the third verse?

What say? Too much khaki? That's just where the fun begins
What about my sister, eh? Just had khaki twins!

Two of the halls Marie played that spring were the Tivoli and the Royal, Holborn. She shared a bill at the Royal with a troop of clog dancers, the Eight Lancashire Lads. It was an unremarkable turn that would have been forgotten long ago, were it not for one of its members – an 11-year-old Charlie Chaplin, the son of music-hall parents. His father, also Charles, enjoyed brief fame before dying of alcoholism at the age of 38. His mother, Lily Harley, had appeared with Marie at a benefit concert at the South London Palace where Marie was just about to embark on her career.[9] Although he appeared on the same bill as Marie at the Royal in 1900, Charlie remembered her best at the Tivoli:

The famous Marie Lloyd was reputed to be frivolous, yet when we played with her at the old Tivoli in the Strand never was there a more serious and conscientious artist. I would watch her wide-eyed, this anxious, plump little lady, pacing nervously up and down behind the scenes, irritable and apprehensive until the moment came for her to go on. Then, she was immediately gay and relaxed. (Chaplin 1964)

Marie certainly suffered from stage nerves. Like all music-hall stars, she could never rest on the success of the latest song. She constantly had to find new material; and she could not be sure she had chosen the right song until she tried it out. On top of this was the need to keep her name continually in the public eye. That was easy enough in London, but regular, lengthy and physically demanding tours round the country were also essential. In 1900, she worked for four months in halls around London. Then, in July, she began a tour that was to keep her on the go until Christmas. Even for a woman of only thirty, the routine was punishing:

| | |
|---|---|
| July: | Empire, Bradford |
| | Empire, Stratford |
| August: | Empire, Sheffield |
| | Empire, Middlesbrough |
| September: | Tivoli, Manchester |
| | Argyle, Birkenhead |
| | Empire, Dublin |
| | Empire, Belfast |
| October: | Empire, Edinburgh |
| | Empire, South Shields |
| | Empire, Newcastle |
| | Empire, Liverpool |
| November: | Palace, Hull |
| | Empire, Leeds |
| | Empire, Bradford |
| | Empire, Birmingham |
| December: | Empire, Bristol |
| | Grand, Hanley |
| | Alhambra, Brighton |

In some of these places, Marie was a guaranteed success, but not everywhere. When she appeared in Bradford in November, the *Bradford Daily Telegraph* carried this report:

> Bradford audiences do not as a rule lavish applause extravagantly even on the most famous artistes and there was last night no deflection at first from the general order of things when Miss Lloyd appeared upon the stage. She returned a Roland for an Oliver, however, (*she gave as good as she got*) by not responding to an encore at the finish.

Audiences at the Ardwick Empire, Manchester, once gave her a rough week. After the second house on Saturday, dressed for her return home, she walked on stage and addressed the empty auditorium: ' "So, this is Ardwick, eh? Well – to hell with the lot of you".' (Jacob 1936)

It was the same at Sheffield. After a particularly turbulent reception from an audience of cutlery manufacturers, Marie strode off-stage, threatening that she would not go on again and making graphic suggestions about what the local people could do with their knives, razors, scissors and circular saws. Someone was sent to her dressing-room to try to calm her down. He eventually succeeded by promising her that the people of Sheffield would do what she said they should with the knives, the razors and the scissors – but, please, could they be excused the circular saws? Marie enjoyed the joke and, at the next house, won the audience over.

Marie also had to prove herself at Edinburgh. In 1900, she was appearing for the first time at the jewel in the crown of the rapidly expanding circuit of music-hall, Moss Empires, founded by Edward Moss. He had begun his career as an entrepreneur in Edinburgh, buying the Gaiety Music-Hall in Chambers Street when he was only 25. Three years later, he took over another theatre at nearby Leith. Before long, he had added theatres in Sunderland, Newcastle and Glasgow to his own personal empire. But he wanted the Edinburgh Empire to be something special. And so it was. Built to the design of the leading theatre architect of the day, Frank Matcham, it presented an impressive display of green, white and gold, the seats in red plush, the boxes adorned with cherubs and nymphs. From its opening in 1892, the Edinburgh Empire was the theatre of which Edward Moss was proudest. But he saw no place for Marie there. The people of Edinburgh disliked vulgarity – he said – and he would take no risks by engaging her. It took eight years for him to change his mind. Marie's fans turned out in large enough numbers to cheer her to the rafters. The *Scotsman* was rather begrudging in its praise: 'She knows how to sing a song well, though her particular class of ballads do not [sic] suit all tastes.' But the *Edinburgh Evening Dispatch* felt readier to enter into the spirit: 'Miss Lloyd excelled, as is her wont, in roguish gaiety and her by-play was immensely tickling.' Moss acknowledged his mistake and booked her again.

# Chapter 14

## 1901

# AUSTRALIA WITH ALEC

The first month of 1901 heralded the end of an era. Queen Victoria, who had been monarch for longer than most people could remember, had been greatly affected by the suffering caused by the Boer War. Her physical health was failing; her sight, in particular, was deteriorating. On 22 January, she died a little short of her eighty-second birthday.[10]

Music-hall had been far beneath her. The closest she came to that rumbustious world was when she heard a tune she liked played by a military band outside Windsor Castle. She sent a lady-in-waiting to find out what it was called. The lady-in-waiting returned, but appeared reluctant to divulge the information. On being pressed, she disclosed that the song in question was 'Come Where the Booze is Cheaper'. The Queen replied: ' "I don't know the meaning of 'booze', though I can guess. But, at all events, the tune is pretty enough".' (*Era* 22 October, 1904)

Marie was in London for only six weeks before leaving Britain for her most far-flung destination yet – Australia. She had a number of new songs to try out. One was another Harrington/le Brunn collaboration, 'Millie!'

Millie isn't silly! Millie is adored!
She's a beautiful high-stepper and they call her extra-pepper
And they say 'Oo-er' when she takes her walks abroad
Millie in Piccadilly fills them with delight
When she walks on terra firma and they see her 'clocks' they murmur
Millie! You're all right!

In another new song, le Brunn set an Edgar Bateman lyric to music. The song was 'Folkestone for the Day':

Twenty ladies, I was one of 'em, all intent on having a spree
Went to Folkestone for a 'oliday, Dabbled our tootsies in the sea
It's a place where costers seldom go
Look on us as low, Stuck up lot, you know
I said Come, girls, we'll upset the show
So, off we started for the day, With all our blokes in tow.
And they 'aven't got over it yet, you bet
We livened up the town
We painted Folkestone beautiful red and came back lovely brown
The would-be-if-they-could-be toffs
They wished us miles away
Oh, didn't we 'ave a pantomime
At Folkestone for the day.

In an interview before leaving for Australia, Marie again talked about the difficulty of picking the right songs:

I am always buying and trying songs, as you may guess. The writers do their best, of course, because they want a success every time, the same as I do. But it does not always come off. A catchy tune, a catchy line, a catchy dance and a catchy dress – well, you say to yourself, this is bound to go. And yet, I have known a song to fail, even under these circumstances. Songs I have had faith in have often disappointed me – songs I did not fancy so much have gone with a 'bang'. (*Era* 9 February 1901)

Preparing for Australia, Marie was packing twenty-one trunks. The interviewer was staggered:

Miss Lloyd is a hard worker and her room, where she does her own dress-making to a very large extent, reminds one of a wardrobe-room at one of the big theatres. Miss Lloyd has been told that she will never live long enough to wear them all and certainly she possesses a tremendous quantity of frocks and skirts of all sorts and sizes, veritably her stage dresses and private dresses are inextricably mixed in the mind of one unaccustomed to such a dazzling and magnificent array of beautiful costumes. (*Era* 9 February 1901)

Marie was booked to appear in Australia by Harry Rickards. In London, he had been a comic singer, specializing in patriotic songs with titles like 'That's the Sort of Man we Want in England Here Today'. But, during the 1860s, he got into financial difficulties. He was declared bankrupt and fled to Australia to avoid his creditors. There, he found success as an impresario, eventually opening the Tivoli in Sydney in 1893 and booking many British music-hall artistes at top rates. In time, he paid back all the money he owed in England and, on his death in 1911, he left about £60,000.

According to Alice Lloyd, Marie was not at first keen to visit Australia. But Rickards made her an offer she could not refuse. ' "Sign up with me for three months and, if you aren't absolutely stuck on the Australians and their country, if you have just one home sickness pang, then I'll release you on a moment's notice and pay you for the full three months." ' (*Lloyds Sunday News* 1922)

Alec Hurley was part of the deal, too. He was to earn £100 a week. Marie's contract was for £250 a week. The couple, travelling as Mr and Mrs Lloyd, arrived at Fremantle. On their first night at the Sydney Tivoli, there was standing room only. Even so, a reviewer for the *Sydney Daily Telegraph* took a high moral tone. 'Marie skates rather close to the brink of what there is a steady determination on the part of theatregoers not to tolerate too much of ... The field of mirth and humour is certainly wide enough to make incursions into the realms of suggestiveness quite unnecessary.' Two weeks later, though the *Sydney Mail* reported: 'Miss Lloyd has established herself as a Tivoli favourite.'

It is difficult to understand why 'Folkestone for the Day' was chosen as a song for Australian audiences. Folkestone must have meant as much to them as Fremantle would have done to British audiences. But luck was on Marie's side. Again and again, audiences called out to her to sing the song – only because the melody reminded them of a song of theirs, 'Molly Doyle'. After Sydney, Marie and Alec went on to Melbourne to open a new theatre for Rickards.

One of Marie's cleverest songs in 1901 was 'Feminine Moods and Tenses', written by Harrington and le Brunn.

When in the near vicinity of any femininity
It's marvellous to note the moods and tenses she'll display
It's first 'I will' and then 'I won't'
And then 'Oh do' and then 'Oh don't'
Sweet woman is as changeable as any April day
Just see her in a milliner's
She's come to choose a hat
'Oh, yes, those toques are all the go this year
Don't you think it's too big, rather?
Wear it back a little farther?
Now do you really think it suits me, dear?
Woman, dear, her moods are rather queer
She often adds a bit to man's expenses
And their husbands – simple ninnies
Buy a hat that costs six guineas
Just to gratify sweet woman's moods and tenses

Back in London, crowds of fans were out in force to welcome Marie home. At the Tivoli, the band played a selection of songs arranged by

George le Brunn and entitled 'Hommage à Marie Lloyd'; at the Oxford, she was presented with bouquet after bouquet; and at the Hammersmith Palace of Varieties, hundreds of people were turned away. Soon after her return, Marie also made a quick trip to Scotland to repeat her success at the Edinburgh Empire.

As soon as she got back from Australia, she found that her dresser and old friend, Bella Orchard, had married. More than once, the Lloyds/Woods had forged links with the horse-racing world. Bella, who was virtually an adopted Wood and had appeared on stage as one of the Lloyds, chose a boxer – in fact, one of the most able boxers of the day, Dick Burge, who, at one stage in his career, had held the British lightweight title.

About a month after the wedding, Dick Burge was arrested for his part in a huge swindle involving the Bank of Liverpool. He was sentenced to ten years' imprisonment. The law was never far from Marie and her circle.

# Chapter 15

## 1902

# A CORONATION REVIEW

The high point of 1902 was the coronation of King Edward VII. After sixty-four years of Victoria, he set a very different style. For a start, he liked enjoying himself and one of the things he enjoyed most was music-hall. Despite his mother's disapproval he had visited the Trocadero and Evans Supper Rooms. He had also attended private parties where the entertainment was provided by his favourite performers, who included Dan Leno, Harry Tate, Arthur Lloyd, Alfred Vance and Jolly John Nash.

Illness delayed the coronation, over which Archbishop Temple officiated, until August. But the Tivoli marked the event in June with a revue, starring Marie and Little Tich.

Revue was still a new entertainment. It made its London début in 1893 when *Under the Clock* was presented at the Royal Court. A young Seymour Hicks, who described it as 'a most impertinent and, at times, rather cruel burlesque' (Hicks 1939), played a leading part in it, impersonating, among others, Dr Watson and an American actor having a stab at Richard the Lionheart, making his entrance with the line 'I am Richard, King of England, and don't you forget it'. Since 1893, revue had made little progress. The format of the Tivoli show even confused the performers themselves, among them the sketch actor George Gray: 'I had carefully watched the rehearsals and had endeavoured to obtain an insight into the plot, but could not trace a vestige. It appeared to be a series of travesties on passing and coming events; nevertheless, it would have compared very favourably with what in later years have been termed revues.' (Gray 1930)

The *Era* also searched hard to define this new-found entertainment: 'Plot is not called for in such a piece and every purpose of a light entertainment is served as long as there is plenty of merry,

MISS MARIE LLOYD AS A MARGATE FATHER.

"THE BATHING PARADE."

irresponsible nonsense, topical bits, burlesque quips and skits on current topics ... We must confess that the humour of these is not always apparent.'

Marie gave a number of impersonations – among them, one of the great French actress Sarah Bernhardt. As it happened, Bernhardt was in London at the time, appearing at the Garrick Theatre. Throughout her career, she enjoyed the strangest of relationships with London's leading costumier and wig-maker, Willie Clarkson. She treated him virtually as her errand-boy, on one occasion ordering him to go to see her in France, as she wanted him to ask W.S. Gilbert to have his one-act play, *Comedy and Tragedy*, translated into French. (Clarkson pleaded with Gilbert, but Gilbert refused.)

Marie had known Clarkson for years. He had designed the costumes for the Drury Lane pantomime in which she had appeared. While Bernhardt was in London, Clarkson arranged for the two women to meet at the theatre at which Bernhardt was appearing. It must have been an extraordinary occasion, both artistes inhabiting such different theatrical orbits. But Bernhardt admired Marie enormously. She described her as a great genius: ' "Now, the two greatest actresses are in the same theatre – but not upon the same stage. You, my dear, are the greatest living comedienne and I, Sarah Bernhardt, am the greatest living tragedienne." ' (*Lloyds Sunday News* 1922)

Of the revue, Alice Lloyd wrote: 'It was a tremendous success; but, strangely enough, it failed financially and had to be withdrawn at the end of the sixth week. There were two causes of this failure – first, the inadequacy of the seating capacity of the old Tivoli; secondly, the enormous pay-roll, which, I have been told, ran into four figures a week!' (*Lloyds Sunday News* 1922)

Although Marie had never met the King, she helped to mark his accession. He gave instructions that, as part of the coronation celebrations, dinners were to be given to more than half a million of London's poor. The dinners, to be held in a number of different meeting-places across the city, were to be accompanied by entertainment organized by a committee headed by Edward Moss. At one of these events, staged at the Floral Hall, Covent Garden, Marie joined Dan Leno, Little Tich and George Robey in providing the entertainment.

Among Marie's new songs in 1902 were two by le Brunn and Harrington. One was 'The Wedding March':

There's bin a reg'lar How-de-do-de-doo this Sunday, boys
For sich a splicing up o' pairs you never saw!
Jest seventeen of us got wed for bett'r or wuss

And we had none of us been never splic'd before
We live in Befnal Green – that's near the Old Red Church, you know
Where they ties all the coster couples up for love
There was fathers, there was mothers
Sisters, uncles, aunts and brothers
In the pewses and the gall'ry up above!

And the weddin' bells were ringin'
And the dicky birds were singin'
As on Sunday mornin' we went away to married be
Arm in arm, as stiff as starch
And we all sang 'Mercy on us'
As the parson smiled upon us
Bill popp'd on the ring and then off to mother's home agen
Why we all done the Weddin' March!

The other le Brunn/Harrington song was of thwarted romance, 'It
Didn't Come Off After All':

Gertie dear's a pretty barmaid,
Who's as tricky as they are made,
Serving in a luncheon bar not far from here
And a reg'lar howling swellah
Little love vows used to tell her
As he whispered in her confidential ear
He said 'When's your night out, ducky?'
Eh? Tomorrow? Oh, that's lucky
Shall I come and meet you, eh, my little pet?
If you'll only say the word, love
I'll take you out like a bird, love
And we'll have a high old time of it, you bet!'

So she donned her best attire, which was something to admire
And she waited for the beau to make a call
But his wife, who'd bowled him, maybe, kept him in to nurse the baby
So, you see, it didn't come off after all.

On 'Do They Do Those Things in London?', Harrington worked
with Albert Perry:

Maudie was a modest little maiden,
Who'd never been to London town;
Never met a masher who was fast or rude
Always wore a silken gown
So, ere she went to London, her ma said:
'Young men are the special things that you must dread!
Never heed the naughty wicked things they say

Else, they're sure to try and kiss you right away'
'Oh! lawks a mussy me! What! they'll kiss me?' said she.
'Do they do those things in London?
Do they really? do they truly?
I never knew they were so wicked
And I'm rather sorry that I bought my ticket
But, still, never mind, I'll rub along somehow
I'm a modest little duck
But I'll chance my luck
I bain't going to turn back now.'

Before the revue, Marie undertook a two-and-a-half month provincial tour:

| | |
|---|---|
| March: | Alhambra, Brighton |
| | Empire, Liverpool |
| | Palace, Manchester |
| | Empire, Bristol |
| April: | Empire, Birmingham |
| | Empire, Leeds |
| | Empire, Bradford |
| | Palace, Hull |
| May: | Empire, Sheffield |
| | Empire, South Shields |
| | Empire, Newcastle |

And, from mid-summer to the autumn, there was another:

| | |
|---|---|
| July: | Empire, Portsmouth |
| August: | Alhambra, Blackpool |
| | Alhambra, Brighton |
| September: | Empire, Edinburgh |
| | Empire, Glasgow |
| | Empire, Liverpool |
| | Empire, Middlesbrough |
| October: | Palace, Manchester |

London dates followed through October, November and December. So, by the time *Aladdin* opened at the Crown Theatre, Peckham, on Boxing Day, she needed a rest. This was, though, her last pantomime ever.

# Chapter 16

## 1903

# ALADDIN AND THE GRAMOPHONE RECORDS

Marie was Aladdin. There was no Daisy or Alice this time. Marie believed in spreading the family favours. Another sister, Rosie, who had adopted the name Lloyd in 1893, was chosen for this pantomime and, according to the *Stage* very charming and pretty she was, too. But it was Marie who proved the draw. The *Stage* reported: 'Where the popular Marie goes, the crowd is sure to follow ... To judge by the enthusiasm manifested on Boxing Day, she has once again taken Peckham playgoers by storm.'

*Aladdin* ran until the end of February. By then, Marie had tried pantomime eight times (once each at Hoxton and Liverpool, three times at Drury Lane and the Crown, Peckham) revue once and musical comedy once. None of these experiments was to be repeated. Marie knew she was at her best as the star turn on a music-hall bill. All the same, she was widely admired by the top men in other theatrical spheres. C.B. Cochran, who became the master of producing revue in London, paid tribute to Marie: 'She was so subtle, the more so because she dealt with obvious things in the subtlest way. Hers was the supreme gift of holding her audience by sheer artistry. She had, beyond every artist that I have ever seen, the supreme talent of timing. The delicacy of her indelicacies was exquisite.' (Cochran 1932)

George Edwardes, who had become a major force behind musical comedy in London, producing a string of successful shows at the Gaiety, Dalys and several other London theatres, offered Marie fabulous sums of money to join his productions, as did Gus Harris's successor, Arthur Collins, who wanted to cast her in a dramatic play, *The Flood Tide*, at Drury Lane in 1903. But, even if Marie had aspired

94

to becoming a Gaiety Girl or a dramatic actress, her contract with the Tivoli prevented her.

She did try something new in 1903. She made her first gramophone records – three of them, in fact, for the Gramophone and Typewriter label. They were all new songs – 'That's How the Little Girl Got On', 'Something on his Mind', and, still capitalizing on her famous wink, 'You Needn't Wink – I know', written by A.J. Mills and Bennett Scott.

> To a seaside spot in Kent
> Sweet young lady and a gent
> Travelled by the five o'clock express from Charing Cross
> As their carriage was reserved
> They felt just a bit unnerved
> When an old boy trotted in and spoilt the fun of course
> The fellow sighed, the lady glared as only ladies can
> The old gent smiled a smile and said
> 'I read your thoughts, young man
>
> You're newly wed, your honeymoon
> And all alone, you'd like to spoon
> You're wishing me to Jericho
> You needn't wink, I know.'

On all three records, Marie was accompanied by an anonymous young pianist whom she congratulated as 'the finest accompanist she had ever had'.[11] (*The Call Boy*, Winter 1987)

Marie tried out another Mills/Scott song that year – 'That Accounts For It':

> Mrs A and Mrs B were discussing over tea
> The usual servant question in a casual sort of way
> Mrs B in tones so sad said 'My servants drive me mad,
> I can't find one that's suitable, now tell me, Mrs A,
> How is it you can always keep your servants?
> We can't get one to stay with us a week.
> I give them decent food and decent wages
> And try to make them happy, so to speak.
> With servants, I have nothing else but worry,
> Yours never seem to trouble you a bit
> Oh, you've got some soldiers' barracks round the corner, close at hand
> Is that so? That accounts for it!

1903 was unusual in that Marie allowed herself, in all, a month's holiday. The Peckham production of *Aladdin* was taken to the Borough Theatre, Stratford, for a week at the beginning of March.

Marie then had three weeks' rest. From the beginning of April, she appeared at a number of London halls before embarking on a two-month provincial tour at the start of June.

| | |
|---|---|
| June: | Palace, Leicester |
| | Empire, Stratford |
| | Empire, Birmingham |
| | Empire, Liverpool |
| July: | Olympia, Newcastle |
| | Empire, South Shields |
| | Empire, Nottingham |
| | Palace, Manchester |

Then, it was back to London for another round of appearances, although they were interrupted by the fourth week's holiday. There was then a second provincial tour, starting in October:

| | |
|---|---|
| October: | Alhambra, Brighton |
| | Empire, Portsmouth |
| | Palace, Southampton |
| | Hippodrome, Hastings |
| November: | Empire, Sheffield |
| | Empire, Edinburgh |
| | Empire, Glasgow |
| | Empire, Middlesbrough |
| | Palace, Bristol |
| December: | Palace, Plymouth. |

Further appearances in London kept her busy until the turn of the year. Marie probably thought nothing of this routine; after all, she had been following it for years. In any case, all music-hall's top-liners drove themselves hard. In 1903, though, worrying news quickly spread through the profession that Dan Leno was suffering a nervous breakdown. He had started having violent rows with his friends – scenes immediately followed by letters of apology. He became prone to locking himself in his dressing room and refusing to come out. When the problems reached crisis point, Dan's wife sent for Arthur Collins, who arranged for him to be admitted to a private clinic. He was seen by a specialist, who forecast that he would recover, but only temporarily. The symptoms would return, although it was uncertain when. The crisis caused great heart-searching at Drury Lane, where Dan was due to play opposite Herbert Campbell in pantomime for the thirteenth successive year. Elaborate preparations were made to cover for Dan, should he not be well enough to appear. But, as predicted, his health improved. He turned up for rehearsals and, when the show

– *Humpty Dumpty* – opened on Boxing Day, a huge roar of joy burst out from Dan's devoted fans. On the last night of the panto, Dan and Campbell made a hopeful prediction in song:

In the panto of old Drury Lane
We have both come together again.
And we hope to appear
For many a year
In the panto of old Drury Lane.

# Chapter 17

## 1904

# BANNED FROM THE COLISEUM

The prediction was not fulfilled. Dan's health broke down again, and, in the hope of finding rest, he went to stay in Bournemouth. One evening, while watching a show at the Winter Garden, he strode onto the stage and shouted at the entertainer in the middle of his act 'Go to your dressing room'. Then, he sat down at the piano and, to the embarrassment of the audience, played five-finger exercises for several minutes. Back in London, he made his way to the bar at the Trocadero one evening and, in front of George Robey, who was drinking there, he started throwing handfuls of sovereigns on the floor. He told Robey he had had hundreds of cottages built in the country for retired performers. 'No more poor pros,' he shouted, 'I have saved them.'

That July, Herbert Campbell suffered an apoplectic seizure from which he never recovered. He died at the age of 57. Dan survived him by three months. He was 43. Marie regarded him as her best friend in the business. She once asked: ' "Ever seen his eyes? The saddest eyes in the whole world. That's why we laughed at Danny. Because, if we hadn't laughed, we should have cried ourself sick." ' (Jacob 1936)

Marie went to Dan's funeral. The same week, Percy Courtenay – after ten years' separation from Marie – petitioned for divorce. Not surprisingly, he named Alec Hurley as the co-respondent.

Perhaps mindful of Dan's fate, Marie took another month's rest from work in 1904. Otherwise, it was the mixture as before: two months' work in London halls at the start of the year; then, in March, four weeks' touring: the Empire, Bradford; the Empire, Liverpool; the Palace, Manchester, and the Empire, Birmingham.

For April, May and June, it was the London circuit again. The holiday came in July. Then, another tour:

September:              Palace, Southampton
                       Palace, Hull
                       Empire, Leeds
October:               Empire, Liverpool
                       Empire, Sheffield
                       Grand, Manchester.


For the rest of the year, Marie was in London. Once again, she had
a number of new songs. One of the more notable ones was 'The Tale
of the Skirt', composed by George le Brunn and Fred W. Leigh:

It is the skirt, you know
That will invariably show
You what the lady is
It never can fail
Everywhere you go
You'll always find that so
It is the skirt, you know, that tells the tale.


The writer Harry Greenwall thought the song was one of Marie's
best:

In this song, she used the art of pantomime to the nth degree. It was a
marvellous piece of acting. In those days, skirts were long and trailing
and they required some manipulation. It was often possible to have
revealed to one a woman's social status by the way in which she
handled her skirts. In this particular song, Marie, without a word, but
with a wink and a flash of an ankle, would leave no doubt in your mind
for a split second that she was one of those ladies who trod the
pavements of Piccadilly late in the evening. (Greenwall 1936)


Another song was a further celebration of Cockney life – 'The
Coster's Christening', written by Harrington and le Brunn:

An' the baby 'e was cryin' like an angel
While old Mother Brown was mopping up the gin
An' they come from near an' far on the noo electric car
Just to see the christening party goin' in
My old mother she was weepin' in the doorway
When the parson come, the kid began to sing
An' we finished up wiv fightin'
So it got a bit excitin'
At the coster baby's christening.

From the 'blue' book came 'Naughty Naughty Naughty', also by Harrington and le Brunn:

> One of them said 'Ah, you may feel proud
> Of presents from lovers sincere
> But the present that Rose got from one of her beaux
> Takes the cake, go on, show it 'em dear.'
> Then the dear little flirt coyly lifted her skirt
> And then said 'Look at the garters Jack bought. He
> Paid two guineas for those'. Then a man shouted 'Rose
> Naughty naughty naughty'.

Marie seemed determined to maintain her reputation for naughtiness, despite the self-cleansing process the halls were now undertaking. A landmark in the abolition of the old vulgarity in the halls was reached towards the end of the year. Alongside Edward Moss, Oswald Stoll was emerging as an important force in theatre management. Like Moss, he started young. He was only twenty-three when he and his mother bought Leveno's Hall in Cardiff and renamed it the Cardiff Empire. Within a few years, he was running eight variety theatres. He eventually joined forces with Moss to form the giant conglomerate, Moss Empires. The opening of the Coliseum in London's St. Martin's Lane on Christmas Eve marked the pinnacle of his career. But, in this theatre at least, Stoll intended to sever all links with the music-hall of the past. In the theatrical papers, notices appeared with this message: 'Coarseness and vulgarity are not allowed at the Coliseum.' In the dressing-rooms, were more notices: 'Please do not use any strong language here.' (Barker 1957).

Stoll, a teetotaller and a non-smoker, had been heard to swear, but only twice. Although he was happy to let Marie appear at any other theatre he owned, she was banned from the Coliseum. Had she been allowed to appear, she would, in all probability, have reacted like the last of the Red Hot Mommas, Sophie Tucker. Before her first appearance in London in 1922, Sophie went to great lengths to study the British sense of humour:

> I was to find out that British audiences love a good bawdy joke ... That goes for all classes and both ends of London. Most of their own performers, who have made themselves tremendously popular with the crowds, have been off colour in their work. Look at ... Marie Lloyd. In Britain, there are some things you can't say in a song without giving offence, such as mentioning a member of the Royal Family. But sex they don't mind. Quite different from the USA, where an entertainer can take all the cracks he wants at the President and other national figures, but brings the wrath of the censor down on him if he mentions some of the well-known facts of life. (Tucker 1948)

The wrath of the censor was brought down on Sophie[12] at the Coliseum. To be more precise, the curtain was brought down on her. She rounded on the censor: 'Mr Stoll, you ought not to be in the theatre. You ought to be a bishop.' (op.cit.)

# Chapter 18

## 1905–6

# THE DEATH OF
# GEORGE LE BRUNN

In January, 1905 Marie played halls in London, and then allowed herself two months' holiday during February and March. Apart from a week at the Ardwick Empire, Manchester, she returned to the London routine from April to July. In August, and part of September, there was a short provincial tour:

| | |
|---|---|
| August: | Empire, Portsmouth |
| | Empire, Nottingham |
| | Palace, Leicester |
| | Empire, Liverpool |
| September: | Ardwick Empire |

She devoted September and October to London halls, but toured outside London again in November: the Grand, Hanley; the Ardwick Empire; the Empire, Leeds; the Empire, Newcastle, and the Olympia, Liverpool.

Then it was back to London for Christmas, and the devastating loss of her main writer. In the week before Christmas, George le Brunn died at the age of 42. He had written the music for nearly all Marie's biggest successes, and had worked for many others besides – Dan Leno, Vesta Tilley, Eugene Stratton, Vesta Victoria, George Robey, Gus Elen, George Lashwood, Alec Hurley, Little Tich, Charles Godfrey and R.G. Knowles.

Many people were surprised that a man of such industry died virtually penniless. But these were the days before the Performing Right Society. Composers still sold their songs to performers outright, and copyright payments, thanks to the work of pirates, were grossly inadequate. In the year of le Brunn's death, his royalties amounted to £1 0s 7d.

The composer Leslie Stuart was particularly incensed:

Mr George le Brunn ... has left a widow absolutely unprovided for. He was admittedly the most prolific popular melodist of the time. His songs are being sung in every corner of the earth and he has probably had more current songs in prominence than any living composer. Through the monstrous depradations of the music pirate he died in financial difficulties. (*Entr'acte* 13 January 1906)

To help le Brunn's widow, a benefit concert was arranged at the Oxford. Many of the stars who had sung his songs appeared – Marie, of course, among them. Marie junior helped to sell the programmes. In all, £600 was raised. In addition, a fund was set up, to which Marie contributed 100 guineas. [13]

Strange to relate, the last song he wrote for Marie marked the beginning of a new phase in her career. She had started out by singing songs in the character of a young girl, and even, in the case of 'Whacky Whack Whack' and 'Johnny Jones', as a schoolgirl. Then she played the part of the knowing young woman, singing songs in which sex loomed large. Le Brunn's last song – with words, of course, by John P. Harrington – moved her on to the role of the mature woman. Although only in her mid-thirties, age was not treating Marie kindly. She had gone from petite to plump. So, as a comedy study, 'You're a Thing of the Past' now suited her well.

On a quiet afternoon in the cosy bar saloon
Of the Mother's Arms, a well-known pub in town
Mrs Green had just popped in for a weeney nip of gin
Strange coincidence – and so had Mrs Brown
One or two small nips and then, Mrs Green she talked like ten
My old man today called me an ugly cat
Ah! But no so long ago, I was beautiful, you know
I remember when he wouldn't have called me that

I was beautiful and fair and I'd lovely golden hair
And a kiss-curl reaching right from here to here
I was called the village star. But the other girl said 'Ah!
That's a thing of the past, old dear'.

With the death of George le Brunn, John P. Harrington needed a new partner. He turned first to James W. Tate, whose background was different from that of most music-hall men. His father had studied music under the Polish teacher Theodor Leschetizky. His sister,

Margaret, shortened her Christian name, misspelt her surname and became the great soprano, Dame Maggie Teyte. James himself was intended for the Church, but chose music instead. At one stage, he was the musical director of the Carl Rosa Opera Company. His first wife was Lottie Collins; his second, the singer Clarice Mayne, whose impersonation of Marie was the only one the Wood family found accurate.

At first, Jimmy Tate appeared on stage merely as Clarice's accompanist. But, as his part in the act grew more important, the couple billed themselves 'Clarice Mayne and That'. He wrote 'I Was A Good Little Girl (Till I Met You)' for her. In 1906, he joined forces with Harrington to produce for Marie 'Customs of the Country':

> In manner orthodox, in England we wear frocks
> That's the custom of the country, don't you know
> In Africa, no doubt, they do all right without
> That's the custom of the country there! Just so!
> In England, every son, of wives has only one
> If you marry more, you're wrong, so there you are
> But, in Persia, married men have at least three score and ten
> If you don't believe me, go and ask the Shah!
>
> It's the custom of the country, very nice custom too
> Marriage is a lottery, there's not the slightest doubt
> Some of them go tying knots and others go without.
> Up in Scotland, they're fond of wedded bliss
> And they're not a bit afraid, no fear
> Courting, marriage, honeymoon, other things occurring soon
> That's the custom of the country here.

Marie saw some more of the country that year, although she spent the first four months touring halls in London. In May, she went north: the Empire, Wolverhampton; the Regent, Salford; the Palace, Grimsby, and the Pavilion, Glasgow.

In June, she was back in London. July was a holiday. Then, another short tour followed: the Empire, Portsmouth; the Hippodrome, Margate; the Alhambra, Brighton; then a week of flying matinees, and finally the Palace, Blackpool.

In the autumn – after years of courtship – Alec Hurley made an honest woman of Marie. Their wedding, held at Hampstead Registry Office, turned into a big music-hall occasion. There were hundreds of letters and telegrams and enough presents to fill two houses. Marie's favourite restaurant, Romano's, supplied a 100-lb wedding cake. Arthur Roberts proposed the health of the happy couple. The female impersonator Malcolm Scott was also on hand with a dreadful riddle:

'Why was Alec Hurley? In order to Marie Lloyd.' (*Era* 3 November 1906)

Alec told the wedding guests he was the proudest man in the world. Marie, who on this occasion gave her correct age, said she hoped to be on the halls for a few more years, then she and Alec would settle down and run a pub. To everyone present there was no doubt that Alec, a modest, mild-mannered fellow, truly loved Marie. For a time, Alec and Marie enjoyed sumptuous, though cosy, domesticity. They had a beautiful home in King Henry's Road. Its centre-piece was the dining room with its Chippendale furniture and blue hangings. With Alec at her side, Marie carried on entertaining as lavishly as ever.[14]

Besides her main home, Marie now had two houseboats, lashed together and moored to the bank on the Thames at Laleham in Surrey. One of the houseboats was called *Sunbeams*; the other, *Moonbeams*. Boating parties often pulled alongside, puzzled by the names. Marie was quite happy to show them round both boats, pour drinks for her sudden guests and explain her choice of names. *Sunbeams* contained the rooms used by day, while *Moonbeams* had the bedrooms.

Marie nearly lost her life one night at Laleham. A heavy mist lay across the Thames as she returned after a trip to the theatre with Alec, Alice and Rosie. Marie went on ahead. But, by the time the others reached the river bank, she was nowhere to be seen. Suddenly, Rosie noticed a bunch of cherries floating on the water – no ordinary bunch, but the cherries that adorned the top of Marie's hat. Alec strode into the water and yanked a bedraggled Marie out. Her reaction: 'What about my Ascot creation? Blimey! It's damn well ruined!' (*Lloyds Sunday News* 1922)

Not many weeks after the wedding, Marie cancelled several performances as the result of illness, the nature of which was undisclosed. Alice stood in for her. Although Marie was rich enough not to worry about the lost income, she did not expect to spell out in public how financially precarious a profession she had chosen; but she had to do that before 1907 was through.

# Chapter 19

## 1907–8

# A PARIS DÉBUT
# AND A TRANSATLANTIC TOUR

Marie – ever the champion of her less fortunate music-hall brethren –
proved just what a valuable friend she could be in the early weeks of
1907. For some time, discontent had been brewing about changes a
handful of music-hall proprietors were making to contracts. For years,
artistes had played one matinee each week as part of the agreed weekly
wage. Suddenly, the word 'matinee' in some contracts became
'matinees', with managers demanding as many as ten performances for
the price of seven. For the stars, the changes did not matter: they just
refused to give extra performances. But rank-and-file entertainers were
not so powerful. They needed the top-liners' support if they were to
put up a successful fight.

Early one morning, a meeting was held at Marie's home in King
Henry's Road to decide what to do. Through the newly formed
Variety Artistes' Federation, a charter of entertainers' rights was
drawn up. With the support of the National Association of Theatrical
Employees and the Amalgamated Musicians' Union, it demanded –
among other things – that an extra twelfth of an entertainer's weekly
salary should be paid for each matinee that was performed. One
manager held out. Walter Gibbons, who controlled the Holborn
Empire, the Islington Empire, the Duchess, Balham, the Grand,
Clapham, the Ealing Hippodrome and the Palace, Croydon, was
prepared to honour the terms of the charter. But he would sign
nothing.

He was given an ultimatum – 4 p.m. on Monday 21 January. The
deadline came and went. That evening, there were no shows at five of
Gibbons' six halls. At the sixth – the Holborn Empire – a pianist
played, a woman sang and a film was shown: *The Alps Seen Through A*

*Telescope.* The next day, the strike spread to the rather larger syndicates run by George Adney Payne and Frank MacNaghten. The manager of the Tivoli received two telegrams from his stars of the week: 'I am learning a new cornet solo. Cannot tear myself away – Little Tich'; 'I am busy putting a new flounce on my dress, so I cannot appear tonight – Marie Lloyd.' (Honri 1973)

At the South London, the manager had only Lockhart's Elephants and a film to show his audience. At one point, he appeared before the curtain: ' "You have had the elephants on once and the pictures once. Would you care to have the pictures again or the elephants? Pictures?" "No!" "Elephants?" "Yes!" The elephants lumbered on – only to be greeted with cries of "Blackleg!" ' (*Performer* 24 January 1907)

As the strike spread, the resolve of the performers strengthened. Fred and Tom McNaughton said: 'These big variety syndicates are treating the small "turns" of our profession worse than serfs' (*Performer* 24 January 1907), and Marie told the *Daily Mirror*: 'Our demands are just. We stand together as a profession. We want to see that everyone concerned with the music-halls receives a living wage. The Labour Party is with us and we shall win.'

Marie even joined a picket line. At one theatre, a second-rate singer called Belle Elmore (real name: Kunigunde Mackamotzki) tried to push her way through. As she did so, Marie shouted to the other pickets: ' "Don't be daft. Let her in. She'll *empty* the theatre." ' (Farson 1972)

The strike lasted three-and-a-half weeks. Three hundred performers came out, together with more than 200 musicians and 90 stage-hands. The dispute was put to arbitration. Marie's evidence at the hearings was particularly interesting. It showed how her salary had risen over the years. In 1889, she had earned from playing *one* hall, £4 a week; in 1896, £25; in 1900, £40; in 1903, £60; in 1907, £80. Marie was music-hall's top earner. By comparison, Little Tich commanded £70; Wilkie Bard £60 and George Robey £25. At the tribunal, Marie was questioned by Walter Payne, Counsel for the Entertainments Protection Association:

*Marie:* That is what I got. That is what I earned. Shall I tell you what I had to spend to get that?
*Payne:* I would rather you did not.
*Marie:* You should see some of my little bills. Will you tell me now then how many months I was off last year?
*Payne:* I do not quite know.
*Marie:* Ah! And my expenses going on just the same.
*Payne:* It was not because you could not get an engagement, was it?

*Marie*: No. That was my illness. But they do not send me anything on Saturday if I do not earn it. (Honri 1973)

Eventually, the arbitration award met most of the Federation's grievances.

Marie was back at work in March. At the end of the month, her daughter, Marie, married Tubby Aylin. The best man was Bernard Dillon, an Irish jockey, who, at the age of 20, was approaching the height of his career. The previous year, he had won both the 1,000 Guineas and the Prix de Paris. Alec introduced him to the family. Marie, for one, was won over by his easy charm.

In May, Marie undertook a short tour: the Empire, Bristol; the Empire, Liverpool; the Ardwick Empire and the Pavilion, Glasgow. Then, in June, Marie made her début in Paris. It took place at the Theatre Marigny, which still stands on the Champs Elysees. Alice wrote:

> Marie knew absolutely no French and, as she sometimes said, when we talked over those hectic days, she thought she was out of luck when she first went to a French restaurant and found that the only two things she could ask for in French were salt and toothpicks! When one considers how entirely British was my sister's performance, how entirely Cockney its appeal, it is really extraordinary that she pleased the French in the way she did; and the Parisians, at that; for they are notoriously critical, not to say blasé. (*Lloyds Sunday News* 1922)

Her biggest success was a new song, 'Tiddley Om Pom Pom', written by Fred W. Leigh and Orlando Powell:

> If you feel an inclination
> To go to Paris to improve your education
> Take advice from one who knows what's what
> You can't learn much there nowadays
> If to see things you've decided
> It would be better if you did what I did
> Take a trip, go to Spain
> When you come back again
> You'll perhaps know what I mean
>
> Tiddley-om-pom tiddley-om-pom Tiddley-om-pom-pom-pom-pay
> Oh the folks they do go on so
> In the land of King Alfonso
> They're a somewhat of a rum lot
> Well, the best thing I can say
> Is Pom-tiddley-om-pom-pom-pom-pom tiddley-om-pom-pom-pom-pay.

Had Marie's knowledge of French been rather more extensive, she might have saved herself a nasty shock during her first performance at the Folies-Marigny. She was so well received that her audience gave her the usual cries of '*Bis, bis*' (Encore, encore!). Marie retired to her dressing-room in great indignation, thinking they were shouting 'beast' at her!

In July and August, she was back in Britain on another provincial tour:

| | |
|---|---|
| July: | Palace, Plymouth |
| | Hippodrome, Eastbourne |
| | Hippodrome, Norwich |
| | Hippodrome, Ipswich |
| August: | Alhambra, Brighton |
| | Hippodrome, Southampton |
| | Hippodrome, Margate |
| | Hippodrome, Portsmouth |

In Norwich, Marie had another reminder that her risquée reputation always went before her. After her Monday afternoon band rehearsal, the manager of the Norwich Hippodrome took her to one side to say: 'I'd just like to point out that this is a Cathedral city and we like to run a family show. So, we don't really want anything that might cause offence.' Marie asked for a railway time-table, so that she could look up the time of the next train back to London. In the event, everything was smoothed over. She gave a performance which, even in a cathedral city, offended no one.

In 1907, both Marie and Alice toured America. Alice's visit was caused by the most extraordinary mix-up, as a result of which she became a star almost literally overnight. Early in the year, the American theatre-owner, Percy Williams, was on the look-out for British stars. He had seen both Vesta Tilley and Vesta Victoria score in America and he wanted to repeat their successes. After contacting his agent in Britain, he was sent a cable: 'Can send Lloyd by next steamer. Am confident she will make big success.' Not unnaturally, Williams thought his agent meant Marie. He cabled back: 'Send Lloyd to open at Colonial immediately on arrival.' (*Brooklyn Daily Eagle* 8 March 1907) This was the Colonial Theatre on New York's Broadway at 63rd Street. Williams prepared bills announcing Marie's first American visit. (Had they been put up, they would, of course, have been wrong. Marie had performed in America in 1890, 1894 and 1897.) But, before they were put up, Alice cabled from Liverpool, announcing that she was about to sail and singing herself '*Alice Lloyd*'.

Back in Williams' office, there was consternation. The advertising bills were destroyed. Another star was booked. And Alice was put on as fifth turn, her time on the programme limited to fifteen minutes.

When she arrived in New York, there was no one to greet her. She went to the Colonial on the following Monday morning and rehearsed her songs with the band. Williams had forgotten all about her – that is, until the first matinee at which she appeared. By the time she reached her third song, the audience were on their feet. Encore followed encore. Fifteen minutes became forty-five. And she was not allowed to leave the stage until she had sung, in all, seven songs.

The Americans liked her lack of brashness. The *Brooklyn Daily Eagle* carried this appreciation: 'Miss Lloyd is of the pink and white, Dresden china type and renders her songs in a dainty, modest and demure manner, instead of hurling them at her audience as we have come to expect from English singers.'

The day after her triumph, she was placed top of the bill, and her name went up in lights outside the theatre. The day after that, her salary was increased from $300 (£60) to $1,500 (£300) a week. Her stay in America was extended to three months. Before returning to England, she signed a five-year contract with the American agents Klaw and Erlanger. Starting in March, 1908, she was to work forty weeks a year in the United States at a salary of $2,000 dollars (£400) a week. Alice expected to make a total of £75,000. With the exception of Harry Lauder, she became the most successful British artiste of her day in America.

All this Marie had to follow. It was not easy. Reviewers whose memories did not stretch back to her previous visit could only compare her with Alice.

Marie and Alec sailed from Liverpool on 26 September, huge crowds of well-wishers seeing them off both at Euston station in London and at Liverpool itself. They arrived in New York on 4 October. The first theatre Marie played was also the Colonial. She sang four songs – 'Customs of the Country', 'Coster's Wedding', 'Tiddley-Om-Pom' and 'Something on his Mind'. If the American show-biz bible, *Variety*, was the first paper she picked up, she must have been downcast: 'The younger sister arrived first in the present-day vaudeville and she stole the cream. It's quite likely that she will keep it ... Alice is more dainty and winsome on the stage.' A week later, it was worse:

> The women of the Colonial audience ... make it unmistakably plain that they do not approve of their English cousin and her naughty songs. Her first three songs passed with rather light applause. When she

finished the Spanish burlesque with its frankly naughty lyrics and its much naughtier wriggles, the men of the audience came to the English woman's rescue and whooped it up in a demand for more of the same sort ... There were probably not half a dozen women in the house that applauded. All of which indicates Miss Lloyd is not going to be the American success her sister, Alice, was. The middle-class American woman is the public dictator in things theatrical and she is not educated to the appreciation of stage humour such as Miss Lloyd's. The London favourite saves herself from downright vulgarity by her wholesome robustness of appearance and bearing.

Marie was not used to criticism, and she took it badly. She booked a page in the *Era* to reprint *Variety*'s review alongside other more favourable criticism. On Christmas Day, 1907, she wrote a confused letter to the founder and editor of *Variety*, Sime Silverman:

Dear Sime, Being Christmas Day, I address you familiarly, knowing full well such action breeds contempt, though that contempt emanates from me. I am sending by same post a copy of the world's greatest variety paper, the *Era*, wherein you will see I reproduce a copy of your well conceived criticism, my one object being that, should the circulation of your paper fail to have reached all whom you desired it to (my friends being far greater than yours), the *Era* would reach them quicker and have more effect, hence I have given your remarks the most prominent position in my advertisement.

In conclusion, let me remind you that 'criticism' is wholesome, at least for the critics, as it helps to relieve the pains of journalistic dyspepsia. Yours, with kind thoughts, Marie Lloyd. (*Variety* 4 January 1956)

It was just as well that other papers took a different line: 'Not only is Miss Lloyd unique, but she is a genius in her way. Compared with her, all the Vesta Victorias and Alice Lloyds became mere imitations.' (*New York Evening Sun*); 'In appearance and accent, she is like her younger sister, Miss Alice Lloyd, only more so. She is plumper and has the same charming smile with the same flash of white teeth – a glaringly British feature – but is more vivacious and acting plays a more conspicuous part in her performance. Her gowns were beautiful and she is one of the nimblest and most graceful dancers ever seen in New York.' (*New York Morning Telegraph*); 'Miss Lloyd is looking younger, if anything, than when she was last here. She wears some stunning gowns and wears them just right.' (*New York Times*)

Two papers gave charming accounts of how Marie must have looked and sounded to new audiences:

An odd little nose perked heavenward; two roguish eyes now blue, now
black; grace, wit, sweetness, tartness, frivolity and earnestness,
tenderness and indifference, immorality without evil – that is Marie
Lloyd, the new [sic] vaudeville star ... In her full, red lips, her plump
little hands, her trim, tight little figure, in her smile, her laugh, in the
toss of her head, in her saucy, swaggering carriage, Miss Lloyd is
intoxicatingly refreshing. (*New York Evening World*)

Miss Marie Lloyd is not a beauty, nor is she a dulcet-voiced singer of
sweet songs. She has an ingrained London face and that peculiar
quality of gritty bawly voice that the London music-hall artist acquires
after shouting for years at the low foreheads of the London 'alls. But she
sings her songs in such rollicking spirits, in such a contagion of good
humour, in such a frolic of light-heartedness, that lo! they leap over the
footlights and you find your own spirits imperceptibly soaring. (*New
York American*)

Marie moved on to one of Oscar Hammerstein's theatres in New
York. But *Variety* continued to pan her, criticizing two of her songs –
'Do They Do Those Things in London?' and 'Eh What What What' –
as being too broad. From New York, Marie travelled to Boston, where
she appeared at Keith[15] and Proctor's theatre on 23rd Street. *Variety*
reported that her act had been emasculated. But she had been allowed
'to keep just enough spice in her business to tickle the male sex'. And
at Christmas, 1907, she was at another of Keith's theatres in
Philadelphia, where *Variety* maintained its campaign: 'Marie Lloyd is
not the dainty stage picture her sister, Alice, is.'
One legend about Marie is that Alice conquered America and she
did not. The truth is that Alice was infinitely more popular in
America than she was in Britain and that Marie was infinitely more
popular in Britain than she was in America. But she *was* still popular
in America; and she does not deserve the verdict handed down by an
American vaudeville expert: 'Our audiences, unaware of her English
reputation ... saw her only as a fattish, middle-aged woman, who sang
songs about rather boring characters and uninteresting locations.'
(Gilbert 1940)
From America, Marie travelled to Canada, where she spent several
weeks. She played just one date – at Shea's theatre in Toronto.
Canadians knew little about her in advance. The *Toronto News*
carried this information: 'Unlike most London concert hall artists,
Miss Lloyd does not pose in male attire.' Having seen her act, the
paper's critic chose not to rave as much as his New York counterparts:
'The most pleasing feature of Miss Lloyd's act is that her methods are
her own. She has a good Cockney dialect when she wishes to use it, a

delightful way of doing French songs and she can take off the demure Yorkshire maiden in a way that wins applause.'

Marie's fourth transatlantic tour finished back in New York, where she again appeared at the Colonial. The *Era* said she received a 'mighty welcome', but *Variety* remained dismissive to the last. It reported that she sang seven songs, including two new ones – 'Don't Grumble at Women Any More' and 'Hulloa Hulloa Hulloa'. But neither, said *Variety*, 'made much headway'.

Marie sailed from New York on 26 February. On her arrival at Plymouth, she told reporters her six months' engagement had been the time of her life.

Apart from appointing a new agent, Harry Day, Marie passed the rest of 1908 relatively quietly, although there were plenty of new songs. One of the most popular was the 'Directoire Girl' by Harrington and Powell.

When they saw me in Directoire Dress
Fellows nearly had a fit. 'Um yes
They all followed up behind in dozens
All the London Johnnies and their country cousins
And they all said Yum yum
I really was a big success
For I showed the fellows more
Than I ever did before
When I put on my Directoire Dress.

Marie took no holiday that year. She appeared at theatres in London, in addition to three forays around the country. In May, she played the Pavilion, Glasgow and the Portsmouth Hippodrome. July saw her in Plymouth, Norwich and Ipswich. And this was the itinerary in October, November and December:

| | |
|---|---|
| October: | Empire, Glasgow |
| | Empire, Edinburgh |
| | Empire, Newcastle |
| November: | Ardwick Empire |
| | Gaiety, Chatham |
| | Palace, Leicester |
| | Empire, Liverpool |
| December: | Hippodrome, Southampton |
| | Hippodrome, Portsmouth |

In October, there was another wedding in the family. While Alice had married one half of a famous comedy double act, Rosie chose the son of one half of an equally well-known act – Will Poluski, who had appeared with his father and brother, the Poluski Brothers, and, at one stage, had been part of Fred Karno's company. It can have been no coincidence that another of Marie's new songs that year was 'Rosie Had a Very Rosy Time', written by Fred Murray and Charles Hilbury:

Rosie had a very rosy time by the ocean blue
Rosie had a very rosy time for Rosie knew the proper thing to do
Every day she paddled in the water in costume sublime
Tho she didn't take her mother
Putting one thing with the other
Rosie had a very rosy time.

# Chapter 20

## 1909–10

# THE MURDER OF BELLE ELMORE

Marie devoted most of 1909 to work, too, taking only a short holiday in Felixstowe in July. Marie loved the seaside. Early in her career, she had sent her family to Southend for a holiday, although, without thinking, she booked only two rooms at a guest house for eleven people. On another visit to Southend, she again displayed her extraordinary generosity. Appearing at the Hippodrome, she saw a party of physically handicapped children in the audience. The following day, she threw a party for them – with cakes and crackers all round. Then, with the approval of the matron of the children's home, she went round with arms full of presents. And, as if that were not enough, she called on the matron again at the end of the week and handed her an envelope. Inside was her week's salary. Occasionally, Alice reminded her that, although she earned a lot, she was by no means a millionairess: ' "Well, what if I'm not? I've got the money and, if I can't spend it how I like, I'll jolly well give up earning more".' (*Lloyds Sunday News* 1922)

In 1909, Marie was taken ill in Southend. She returned home, where she underwent an operation. No detail was given, other than a reference to an internal complaint. It was to recuperate from the operation that she took herself to Felixstowe.

On the brink of 40, she was singing more 'old maid' songs. The gradual change in her act failed to stop the Mrs Grundys making a fuss. In the autumn, someone complained to the London County Council about her routine at the Chelsea Palace. The Council launched an investigation. But Marie was unstoppable.

Again, it was a year spent mostly appearing at London theatres. But there were quick trips outside the capital: in March, to Glasgow; in April, to Exeter; in May, to Cardiff. In August, she appeared in

Margate, Southampton, Portsmouth and Nottingham; in September, in Birmingham; and in October, in Plymouth. Also in October, the Music Hall Ladies Guild, which Marie had helped to found, held its second annual dinner. It was now going strong, helping dozens of deserving families each year. Marie was no longer President. That honour fell to the wife of the King Rat, Fred Ginnett. At the dinner, a presentation was made to the treasurer, Belle Elmore, the singer about whom Marie had been so rude during the strike. Belle made an unassuming speech. She said she enjoyed her work and hoped to be able to continue doing so.

Belle could not fulfil her wish. 1910 saw both her and Marie in marital difficulties. Marie and Alec – so in love at one time – had drifted apart. There was more than one reason. Offstage, Marie had a quiet side to her nature. In private, she was quite an ordinary woman. She was always out of bed by nine in the morning. She read newspapers, but never books. She rarely wrote letters. She wrote only once to Alice – to tell her about the birth of Myria. She loved housework and sometimes, on returning from an evening's work on the halls, she did not even remove her stage clothes and jewellery before setting about cleaning out cupboards. Before she had a pony and trap, she went for long walks in the country and looked round churches. After she had bought a car, she went regularly to Brighton – partly for the sea air, but also so that she could go to the races at Kempton Park. She laid bets, but usually lost. In fact, towards the end of her life, she lost a lot. She also played solo whist, but not well; she tended to overbid. Her other game was golf, but, as she said herself: 'I don't play golf. I play at it.' (*Lloyds Sunday News* 1922) As for the legitimate theatre, she went irregularly – her favourite night out being a full-blooded melodrama at Drury Lane. She ate simply. Although she went to Romano's, it was not for the lavish food, but for the company. This was not Alec's style. He would have preferred the quiet life all the time. Also, successful though he was, he achieved nothing like the stardom Marie enjoyed, and that caused resentment. The main problem, though, was Bernard Dillon. He had lavished attention on Marie, and she was flattered. By February, Alec had had enough. He filed for divorce, citing Dillon as the co-respondent. But, when the case reached court, neither Alec nor Marie appeared. The petition was struck off.

Belle Elmore's problems were rather more acute. At the start of February, the Music Hall Ladies' Guild received a letter purporting to come from her, saying she was resigning as she had to go to the United States at short notice. The Guild's officers were mystified, as the letter appeared to be a forgery. For a start, her surname was spelt with two l's instead of one.

At the end of February, Belle's husband[16] attended the annual dinner of the Music Hall Railway Association, accompanied by his secretary. She had been born Ethel Neave, but she called herself Ethel le Neve. There was further mystery when those present at the dinner – among them, Alec Hurley – noticed that Ethel was wearing Belle's sealskin coat and some of her jewellery.

At the end of March, the *Era* printed a death notice: 'Elmore March 23 in California, U.S.A. Miss Belle Elmore'. Shocked by that bald announcement and what had occurred previously, one of the Guild's vice-Presidents went to the police to voice her suspicions. But she was told that, unless she made a charge, nothing could be done. Between March and July, a friend of Belle's – a theatre manager, John Nash, the husband of the singer, Lil Hawthorne – went to America. While there, he tried to find out more about her death, but without success. On his return, he went to see Belle's husband, who insisted that, while abroad, she had been taken seriously ill with pneumonia and had died. Nash was not satisfied with the explanation. He, too, went to the police. At the beginning of July, they went to see Belle's husband at his home at Hilldrop Crescent, Finsbury Park, where Ethel le Neve was now living.

Belle's husband admitted that he had lied. He now said that he and Belle had quarrelled and that she had left him. Meanwhile, Ethel told her sister that the police did not believe him. The two of them were going to America, she said, to try to find the man who was supposed to have sent the cable saying Belle had died.

The same day, the couple went to Willy Clarkson's shop, saying they wanted to play a hoax on some friends. Ethel was kitted out as a boy. The couple travelled to Brussels where, three days later, they booked a voyage to Quebec on board the *Montrose* as Mr and Master Robinson.

The following day, Belle's remains, mutilated almost beyond recognition, were found at Hilldrop Crescent.[17] Her husband, who had had a medical training, but who worked as an agent for quack medicines, had given her a powerful narcotic poison, hyoscine hydrobromide, and had hacked her to death. The papers were full of the grisly murder.

A hundred and fifty miles off the Irish coast, the captain of the *Montrose* sent a wireless message to Scotland Yard, saying he believed he had Belle's husband and Ethel le Neve on board. The police gave chase. A Scotland Yard inspector left Liverpool on a liner faster than the *Montrose* and, off the coast of Quebec, arrested Belle's husband. This was the first time the wireless had been used to intercept a criminal.

In November, at the Old Bailey, Ethel le Neve was charged with being an accessory to murder. She was acquitted. Belle's husband – Hawley Harvey Crippen – was found guilty of murder and was hanged.

The following month, anyone who had failed to realize that, after two husbands, Marie had a new man in her life, learned of the fact in a very public way. Bernard Dillon reached the climax of his racing career by winning the Derby in record time. Marie was there to cheer him on.

Further literary judgment was passed on Marie in 1910. Shaw and Beerbohm had already had their say. One night, Arnold Bennett was in the audience at the Tivoli. He did not think much of Marie:

> Little Tich was very good and George Formby, the Lancashire comedian, was perhaps even better. Gus Elen I did not care for. And I couldn't see the legendary cleverness of Marie Lloyd. She was very young and spry for a grandmother. All her songs were variations of the same theme of sexual naughtiness. No censor would ever pass them, and especially he wouldn't pass her winks and her silences. (Bennett 1932)

He was entitled to his opinion. But his facts were wrong. Marie was no grandmother!

Chapter 21

1911–12

# THE ROYAL COMMAND
# PERFORMANCE

Marie spent the first few months of 1911 in South Africa. This time, it was just a holiday, though one appearance at the Johannesburg Empire was scheduled.

With the accession of George V, royal recognition of music-hall took another step forward. The owners and managers of most of London's leading halls invited him to command – as they put it – a music-hall performance, either in London or Edinburgh. The King agreed, choosing Edinburgh as the venue and July as the date. And so, plans were made for the first Royal Command Performance. But it was not staged in July of *that* year. Neither was it staged in Edinburgh.

At Moss's favourite theatre, the Edinburgh Empire, a German magician and illusionist, known as the Great Lafayette, was appearing with his 40-strong company and a number of animals. During the turn, a flaming torch, which Lafayette was holding above his head, set fire to one of the drapes. At first, the audience thought it was part of the act. But the flames quickly spread to other curtains and scenery. To try to avert panic, the orchestra played the National Anthem and the safety curtain was lowered. As the fire took hold of the theatre's roof, the audience filed out into the street. There was apparently no panic, the audience left as quickly as they could. None of them was killed. But Lafayette and several members of his company lost their lives. The Royal Command Performance was postponed.

In 1911, Marie took no holiday at all, although she missed performances at the Hippodrome, Boscombe, and the Empire, Leeds, because of illness. Out of London, she did appear at the Hippodrome, Portsmouth; the Hippodrome, Southend; the Hippodrome, Margate and the Empire, Nottingham. Her main song was 'Put On Your Slippers', written by Harrington and Orlando Powell:

> Put on your slippers, you're in for the night
> Stir up the fire and turn down the light
> Don't let me spoil your yum-yum, chum
> Call me when the milkman comes
> So, put on your slippers, you're in for the night.

On the one hand, the song could conjure up a charming, domestic scene. On the other, it could sound like an invitation to infidelity. It was that sort of lyric the organizers of the Command Performance had in mind when they drew up the list of entertainers they wanted in the show.

The Command Performance was finally fixed for the Palace Theatre in London in July. But, when the committee announced the entertainers who had been chosen, there were surprising omissions. Eugene Stratton had been left out. So had Albert Chevalier. And so, too, had Marie. She was uncharacteristically quiet about the decision. But Chevalier, whom Marie had helped on his début on the halls, voiced his disappointment. He suspected his name had not even been submitted to the King, even though he had appeared before him at Sandringham. He was also angry about the snub to Marie.

> Who is there more representative of the variety profession? Miss Lloyd is a great genius. She is an artist from the crown of her head to the sole of her foot. You know the range of my theatrical experience, the actors with whom I have been associated and the parts I have played. Well, I say deliberately that no woman alive can 'read' a song like Miss Lloyd – can get so much out of the lines. It is an education to hear her. (*Era* 22 June 1912)

Three possible reasons were put forward for Marie's omission. First, her private life: she had lived openly with Alec before her divorce from Percy Courtenay. She was now living openly with Dillon while still married to Alec. Second, her reputation for being rude made her too much of a risk in front of royalty. Third, theatre owners and managers were getting their own back on her for helping to organize the 1907 strike. A look at the list of men on the committee arranging the Command Performance shows who Marie was up against. [18] Besides Moss, Stoll and Walter de Frece, there was Walter Gibbons, the first man to feel the strikers' wrath. But then W.H. Clemart, of the Variety Artistes Federation, was also on the committee, as was the

sketch and song writer Wal Pink, who had provided material for
Marie. In addition, Little Tich, Gus Elen and the McNaughton
Brothers, all of whom had stopped work in 1907, were chosen. The
truth is that Marie was probably left out for a mixture of these three
reasons.

Again, Marie took no holiday in 1912. And again, she was ill,
forced to miss shows at the London Pavilion and the Empress,
Brixton. She did, though, get to Paris again – this time, for a longer
visit. She had a clutch of good new songs that year, including one in
praise of Paris, written by Powell and Leigh, 'I'd Like To Live In Paris
All The Time':

See the twinkle in me eye?
Just come back from France, that's why
Me and Bill went over there to spend our honeymoon
Fust time, me, in foreign parts
Did I like it? Bless yer hearts
Can't say more about it than it ended up too soon.
Don't think I'm done wi' good old England – not likely
Born and bred down Hackney way and proud to own it too.
How's the make-up? Ain't it great?
Latest thing from Paris – straight!
Gives a gal a chance to show what she can do.

Oh! I'd like to go again
To Paris on the Seine
Paris, it's a proper pantomime
If they'd only shift the Hackney Road and plant it over there
I'd like to live in Paris all the time.

Marie also underlined her love of London in the 'Piccadilly Trot',
the melody of which made half a concession to the growing popularity
of ragtime. It was written by George Arthurs and Worton David:

Lately you have heard about the Turkey Trot
Some say it's rot, some say it's not
But I've got another one that beats the lot
Doesn't come from Yankeeland
If you see a Johnny in the latest style
Money a pile, glossy new tile,
With a swagger you can see for half a mile
You will quickly understand

It's the Piccadilly Trot, trot, trot, trot

Now the rage in town
It's the Piccadilly Trot, trot, trot, trot
See 'em strolling up and down
With a pretty little girl, what, what, what!
It's a trifle hot, Great Scot
It's fine, fine, simply divine
Grab yourself a girlie and get right into line
That's the Pic-Pic-Piccadilly Trot.

On the night of the Royal Command, Marie was not far from Piccadilly. She was playing the Pavilion, where she had threatened to put up placards announcing 'Every performance by Marie Lloyd is a performance by Command of the British Public'. As it turned out, the Royal Command was a bit of a flop. Most of the participants were riddled with nerves – Little Tich so much so that he refused to go on at the end. All the same, King George and Queen Mary expressed their delight, referring to the entertainers' talent as 'equal in excellence and varied in style'. But Marie was probably well out of it. Her non-appearance certainly did her no harm.

She spent most of her year in London, but also fitted in the following itinerary:

| | |
|---|---|
| March: | Empire, Edinburgh (newly rebuilt after the fire) |
| | Empire, Newcastle |
| | Pavilion, Glasgow |
| April: | Empire, Liverpool |
| May: | Empire, Birmingham |
| August: | Hippodrome, Margate |
| | Hippodrome, Boscombe |
| | Hippodrome, Exeter |
| October: | Pavilion, Glasgow |
| November: | Palace, Manchester |
| December: | Olympia, Liverpool |
| | Empire, Sunderland |

After all the songs about her famous wink – and in the year which saw her banned from entertaining royalty partly as a result of her so-called suggestiveness – she had a new lyric, which, more than any, summed up her style. It was 'Every Little Movement', written by F.E. Cliffe and C.J. Moore:

Every little movement has a meaning of its own
Every little movement tells a tale
When she walks in dainty hobbles
At the back round here, there's a kind of wibble wobble

And she glides like this
Then the Johnnies follow in her trail
Cos when she turns her head like so
Something's going, don't you know
Every little movement tells a tale.

Chapter 22

1913–14

# TROUBLE IN AMERICA
# AND A THIRD WEDDING

The year 1913 saw Marie preparing for her fifth trip to America – 25 weeks, booked by the Orpheum Circuit and United Booking Offices, at $1,750 a week. It was to be her most extensive tour and, as it turned out, her most controversial. She and Bernard Dillon sailed from Britain on board the *Olympic* on 24 September. Alice was on the quayside in New York to greet them on their arrival on 1 October.

Marie, having been given her landing papers, passed through Customs. She sent her maid on to the Astor Hotel with some luggage. But, while waiting for another trunk, she and Alice stayed on the wharf. While they were there, an English journalist came up for a chat. He was surprised to see her because, as he pointed out, he had not seen her name on the passenger list. It was then that Marie admitted that she and Dillon had travelled as husband and wife. The journalist said his goodbyes, but, before he left the quayside, he told the authorities what he had learned.

American immigration officials then came to hear Marie's version. She told them she was not Dillon's wife in law, but she was in fact. She also asked – in vivid language – what it had got to do with them. There was a great deal of discussion, at the end of which Marie was told that she could be admitted to the United States, but that Dillon would have to return to England. She refused and returned to the *Olympic*, where a conference was held in the captain's cabin.

Marie insisted that she would appeal against the officials' decision. For the first night of her visit, she was allowed to stay on the ship. But, the following morning, the officials came back on board to say she would have to be treated like all other undesirable immigrants. She would be detained on Ellis Island, where a grim-looking, antiquated building temporarily housed would-be immigrants. Alice wrote: 'Imagine the position. There was my sister, exquisitely gowned, turned loose in a long shed filled with wretched emigrants in all stages of disease and dirt. There was a great stove and, from this, the place became horribly overheated and malodorous.' (*Lloyds Sunday News* 1922)

After a few hours, the Governor rescued her and allowed her to use his private apartment. Even so, she was locked in and a wardress was placed at the door. After the second night of her visit, Marie pulled up the blind: 'Standing out more prominently than any landmark, there was that great Statue of Liberty. Well, I felt so wild, I banged down the blinds and swore I'd go back on the *Olympic*, whatever Washington said.' (*Lloyds Sunday News* 1922)

Marie booked her cabin. But, a few hours before she was due to sail, the result of the appeal came through. She and Dillon were to be allowed to stay, providing she returned to Britain as soon as she had finished her tour. In addition, she and Dillon would have to live apart.

Marie's troubles quickly became headline news both in London and New York. The *New York Sun* said the authorities were straining at a gnat and swallowing a camel. In Fleet Street, the *Daily Sketch* was more forthright:

> The United States is the home of the cheap, nasty divorce. Its cities are hotbeds of vice, its dances the latest thing in vulgarity and ugliness and it has just decided that Marie Lloyd is not a fit and proper person to land upon its sacred shores ... Let the Yankee keep his sanctimonious humbugs for home consumption ... Hands off the English, if you please.

There was also criticism of Marie's employers. Neither Martin Beck, of the Orpheum theatres, nor Edward Albee, of UBO, had been to see her. The only statement they issued was this: 'This sort of publicity is very distasteful to us.' (*Variety*) But the publicity had one positive effect. By the time Marie reached the brand-new Palace Theatre in New York, there was not a spare seat in the house. Sime Silverman, who wrote *Variety's* review himself, had changed his tune since Marie's previous visit:

> Miss Lloyd's songs, which, four [sic] years ago, would have been termed suggestive, are really very mild. When one recalls the daring (and worse) 'rag' songs, the lewd dances, the tainted sketches and everything unclean big time vaudeville has stood for of late to hold up the box office, Miss Lloyd, with her stories in lyrics that have a laugh in every verse and chorus, is an object lesson to American vaudeville managers. It should teach them the art of being funny without being dirty.

By the end of October, Marie was doing so well, the Palace put up its seat prices. From New York, Marie moved on to Keith's theatre in Cleveland, Ohio. After that, she was due to appear in Cincinnati. But the train from Cleveland ran into snow drifts. Marie returned to New York – and more problems.

It appeared that a clause in her American contract allowed her bookers to send her wherever they wanted. Marie had expected some dates for the first time in the Western half of the country. Instead, it looked as though she was to appear solely in the east. At the end of November, she pulled out of the bill at the Orpheum, Brooklyn, objecting to opening the second half of the programme. For the remainder of the week, she 'rested'. By the end of that week, some Western dates had been found for her.

For her American audiences, Marie sang mostly songs that had already proved successful in Britain. But she did have one new song in 1913 – 'My Actor Man', which James W. Tate wrote with Clifford Harris:

> My actor man! My actor man!
> Such a gentlemanly fellow
> With a voice so deep and mellow
> How he talks! The way he walks!
> He simply is a treat that can't be beat, he's grand!
> His actor clothes – his actor pose
> And everything about him's idealistic
> And oh! when he makes love to me
> Well, everything he does is so artistic.

Alec Hurley was not an actor. Neither was he, by now, Marie's man. But it is odd that Marie should have sung her only love song to a man of the theatre at this time, unaware of what was happening back home. Since breaking up with Marie, Alec had been drinking heavily. At the end of November, he was taken ill while appearing in Glasgow. On his return to London, an attack of pleurisy was diagnosed, complicated by pneumonia. In the early hours of 6 December, he died at the age of 42, apparently pledging his love for Marie to the end.

Her family attended his funeral in force. They had liked Alec for his sincerity. They also recognized that, of the three men in Marie's life, he was the only one who treated her properly. The news was broken to Marie in Chicago. She soon recovered from the shock. Two days after Alec's death, she opened at the Palace, Chicago. *Variety* reported that she lived up to expectations: 'Her routine of gingery lyrics seemed fully appreciated by the capacity house.'

Oddly enough, it was not quite the same at the Majestic in the same city the following week: 'Marie Lloyd did not have an easy time of it. She did not elicit much laughter with her songs and it was not until she got into her imitation of an English coster girl that she really aroused enthusiasm.' (*Variety*)

At the turn of the year, Marie was in St Louis, Missouri, and Milwaukee. Then, she crossed into Canada. On 12 January, 1914, she opened at the Orpheum, Winnipeg. The *Manitoba Free Press* reported: 'Her hold upon her audience is so strong as to make satiety impossible'. But from there, things got worse. In Regina, her songs were severely criticized. Church leaders, in particular, took a strong line. Marie, in turn, was unimpressed by Regina. Asked about the ministers' reaction, she said the only trouble they had previously given her was when she had fallen asleep in church. Being mid-winter, the temperature in Regina was 40 degrees below zero. Most of the town's people went to bed early. The dining room of the hotel, where Marie stayed, closed at seven in the evening. After seven, the town was dead. But the theatre was always full. In a contentious interview in the *Vancouver Sun*, Marie commented: 'Where the h—— do they all come from? I don't know. They must have come out of 'oles like a lot of rats.'

Marie reached Vancouver itself at the beginning of February. At the Orpheum, she was given a great welcome. The *Vancouver Sun* reported that there was 'immense enthusiasm on the part of appreciative patrons, who filled the house from floor to gallery'. Marie was 'called before the curtain so many times that even the management lost count and the "gods" bellowed themselves hoarse'. Local paper reviewers, though, took a different view. The *Vancouver World* said: 'People here do not care for the sort of stuff which appeals strongly to Seven Dials or Billingsgate'; and the *Daily News Advertiser* reported: 'That, in the opinion of many, she seriously mars the talents she possesses by introducing into her songs much that is suggestive in word and gesture, but particularly in word, is regrettable.' (*Vancouver World* 9 February 1914)

The Mayor of Vancouver agreed with the papers. He ordered the theatre's management to cut two of Marie's songs – some accounts said three songs, although it's not known which. The management's response was that, once Marie was on stage, she was out of their control. Squaring up for a fight, Marie said she would give Vancouver 'something to think about' at her last performance there. As a result, the civic dignitaries panicked. The Mayor cancelled Marie's last performance altogether because of 'threats [she had] made to indulge in personalities on the stage and the fact that she had not cut out suggestiveness in her songs'. (*Vancouver Sun* 9 February 1914). It did not end there. Marie still went on stage to try to explain herself. But she broke down in tears instead. It had not been an easy week. The press were almost uniformally hostile. The *Vancouver World* took her to task for the language she used:[19] 'Any person who has ever heard what Marie Lloyd says when she becomes peeved always falls back in disorder. Her language is strong. It is livid, cantankerous, biting and has the same effect on human feelings as sulphurated hydrogen has on the olfactory organs.'

Marie had some excuse. During her week in Vancouver, she learned that, by crossing into Canada, she had forfeited the opportunity to return to the United States. American officials argued that, under the terms of the bonds negotiated in Washington, as she was once again on British soil, she would have to stay there. Had the United States stuck to its decision, Marie would have had to cancel several further engagements in America: 'One would think I was a murderess or some criminal. I would think they would be glad to have a woman as decent as I am in their country.' (*Vancouver Sun* 3 February 1914)

Another immigration hearing was held – this time in Vancouver. Again, Marie had to promise that she would leave America as soon as she had completed her engagements. Dillon was also barred from travelling with her. At first, Marie would not go without him. But she changed her mind. She was glad to see the back of Vancouver.

Before she left, there occurred another of those incidents of which Marie Lloyd legends are made. The story is that Marie was so annoyed with one of the newspaper reviews of her that she went to the office of the editor who printed it and horse-whipped him. This is the evidence. Marie *was* annoyed at the way her remarks about Regina had been printed in the *Sun*. She sent the editor an unpunctuated and (again) confused letter: 'To Editor Sun Newspaper Vancouver Hell is spelt with an H and I aspirate mine in future and send intelligent men to interview clever women especially an Englishwoman like Marie Lloyd'

She also said she would like to knock the *Sun*'s reporter on the nose. But there was no mention of horse-whips. The *Advertiser* reported that Marie had stormed into the office of the editor of the *World*: 'Swinging a strap, it is alleged, she was bent on giving satisfaction, when the editor left his office and summoned a police officer. When the constable arrived, the lady had left the building.'

There again, no horse-whip; and the alleged strap was not even used. But the horse-whip story was printed in London and New York. Marie often complained that papers printed false stories about her. But she was not above encouraging them when it suited her.

From Vancouver, Marie travelled to Seattle. On 16 February, she opened at the Orpheum at Portland, Oregon. On 20 February, Dillon caught up with her. And on 21 February, they married at the British Consulate, Marie describing herself as a vaudeville actress and giving her age as 32, a full twelve years short of her real age.

There was no romance about the wedding. In London, the *Era* reported that 'the ceremony was performed to obviate further difficulty with the American immigration authorities'. In Portland, Marie gave an interview to the *Morning Oregonian*:

> If I had only known it, Mr Dillon and I could have been married in Canada and I'd have had no bond to put up for him, but we did not want to get married and had no idea the authorities would hold him … He is a Roman Catholic and I'm a member of the church whose creed is 'Do as you would be done by.' And I hope they are satisfied when I've got my little piece of paper saying I'm respectable. I ain't no hypocrite. I don't smoke – but I know 50 women who condemn it in public and sneak a puff in quiet. I like a drink when I want it – sociable like – but I does it open and above aboard. I know hundreds who get theirs in teapots.

Marie went on to make an astonishing claim against Alec – an allegation that appeared almost callous only ten weeks after his death:

> I do not see how marrying Mr Dillon is going to make any difference, only that I might like him less. I know that the quickest way to lose your pal and friend is to marry him. I lived with my second husband for ten years before I married him and, in two weeks after we trailed up the altar, he was smiling at another.

Marie was back in broad-minded territory. At the beginning of March, she began a fortnight at the Orpheum, San Francisco, where she was cheered to the rafters. The *San Francisco Chronicle* reported: 'Méchante Marie and her air of diablerie … were assorted for resistance and early her audience capitulated to these and those naughty little songs that she sends wafting across the footlights with all the teasing witchery at her command … Her gowns were a revelation – in more ways than one.'

There soon began the long haul back to the east coast, playing at Salt Lake City and Denver, Colorado, *en route*. In New York, something of a publicity stunt had been arranged. On the same day in May, Marie was to open at Hammersteins on 42nd Street and Alice was to open at the Palace on the opposite corner. There was, of course, no rivalry between them. In fact, on their last night, Marie finished her act first and crossed to Hammersteins, just as Alice was singing the most famous song of her career, 'Splash Me'. At the back of the stage, where Alice could not see her, Marie started mimicking her every movement. The audience loved it – the two famous Lloyd sisters together on a New York stage, a far cry from the Fairy Bell Minstrels nearly 25 years before.

Alice set sail for England on board the *Lusitania*. (This was just a year before the ship was torpedoed off the Irish coast with the loss of 1,200 lives.) Marie set sail on 30 May on the *Olympic* – the liner that had brought her to the middle of all her trouble eight long months previously.

# Chapter 23

## 1914–19

# THE FIRST WORLD WAR

On her return to Britain, a reporter asked Marie whether she would ever visit America again: 'My reply ... cannot be better expressed than in the now well-known response given in Bernard Shaw's much-discussed phrase lately spoken by Mrs Patrick Campbell as Eliza Doolittle in *Pygmalion* at His Majesty's.' (*Era* 12 August 1914)

Marie's fifth American tour was, in fact, her last professional foreign trip anywhere. Within two months, the face of the world began changing. From the beginning of August, Britain and Germany were engaged in a war, which, over the next four years, was to spread worldwide and claim nearly 10 million lives.

Anti-German feeling ran high. To counter Leichner stage make-up, Willy Clarkson put on the market Clarko, 'the all-British greasepaint, superior in every way to the German article'. The product was exalted by Marie in newspaper adverts: 'I can highly recommend your all-British greasepaint.'

Box office receipts were soon hit, as people decided to stay at home rather than risk a night out on the town. Before long, London managements were negotiating with the Variety Artists' Federation over how to keep the halls going.

Characteristically, Marie's thoughts turned to helping the men called to war. She proposed a series of shows, the proceeds of which would provide 'creature comforts for our gallant London Territorials, now detailed to defend our shores from our German foes'.

From her houseboat at Thames Ditton, Marie planned further creature comforts. Alice wrote:

I recall one occasion when she gave a treat to the boys in blue from the Hammersmith Hospital. She chartered seven motor lorries at her own expense to bring the men along to the Albany Hotel, Thames Ditton. She hired the complete orchestra from the Oxford music-hall and she had the whole of the hotel grounds arranged for the poor fellows. After the concert, there was a trip up the river in specially chartered motor-boats, then a huge 'blow-out', not forgetting cigarettes and tobacco. (*Lloyds Sunday News* 1922)

Such generosity was entirely in line with Marie's credo, 'A Little Of What You Fancy Does You Good', a thought couched in song for her by Arthurs and Leigh:

I always hold in having it, if you fancy it
If you fancy it, that's understood
And suppose it makes you fat
I don't worry over that
Cos a little of what you fancy does you good.

Marie's beneficence was not just confined to London. Alice Lloyd again:

It was the same in every provincial city in which she appeared throughout the war – in Glasgow, Edinburgh, Birmingham, Newcastle, Dundee, Birkenhead, Hull, Bath, Swansea and in other places, which I forget. A considerable portion of her salary went to the wounded, but she wanted no other thanks than the happy faces of the men themselves. (*Lloyds Sunday News* 1922)

In addition, Marie took part in Sunday evening 'Concerts for the Troops' at the Princes Theatre in Shaftesbury Avenue, organized by Seymour Hicks. Collins and Leigh provided her with a morale-boosting song, 'Now You've got Yer Khaki On':

I do feel so proud of you, I do honour bright
I'm going to give you an extra cuddle tonight
I didn't like yer much before yer joined the army, John
But I do like yer, cocky, now you've got yer khaki on.

Marie's love of khaki did not extend to her husband. Bernard Dillon appealed to the Hendon tribunal for exemption from military service. He told the panel that he used to earn good money from racing, but he was now too heavy and was earning his living chiefly from dealing in horses. He insisted he had to support not only his parents but four brothers, too. He was refused exemption.

Dillon had grown fat because he drank too much; and his drinking induced violent tempers. Marie had married another wife-beater. One day, Ada Reeve ran into Marie, who was trying to conceal a black eye with make-up and a heavy veil: ' "Have you had an accident, Marie?" I asked solicitously. "Accident my foot" (It was another part of the body she mentioned … As I have hinted, Marie had a ripe vocabulary.) "*He* did it, the so-and-so".' (*Lloyds Sunday News* 1922)

As well as entertaining the troops, Marie had to boost her fans' morale as well. During one of the Zeppelin air raids, she was playing the Woolwich Hippodrome. In the interval, when the curtain was down, the big naval guns began to sound nearby. Panic soon gripped the audience. It looked as though they were preparing for a hasty exit. But Marie saved the situation. She stepped in front of the curtain and, speaking as loudly as she could, made this announcement: ' "If some of us are going to get it, then let's all get it together. Meanwhile, if you will take your seats again, I will sing you a song or two." ' (*Lloyds Sunday News* 1922) The audience did what they were told.

During the war, the music-halls suffered another attack of Puritanism. The London Council for the Promotion of Public Morality, voicing fresh concern about the moral standards of acts on the halls, sent a delegation to the London County Council. The controversy over promenades also resurfaced. A few months before the war, the Bishop of London, Arthur Foley Winnington-Ingram, had preached at St Mary's le Strand: 'It is not that the church expects every music-hall to produce a sermon night after night. [But] those who go … should find nothing to make their girls blush or stain the imagination of their boys.' (*Era* 25 February 1914) As for the promenades, the Bishop leaned heavily on the LCC: 'There are a large number of women of doubtful character in these promenades every night and … they are a constant danger and temptation to the young men who naturally wish to have some amusement after a hard time in the trenches or a long sojourn in some camp at home.' (*The Times* 18 July 1916)

To those whose memories went back twenty years, it was all *déjà vu*. This time, though, there was no Winston Churchill to lead the cause. He was in command of the sixth battalion, Royal Scots Fusiliers, in France. The London County Council added a quaint line to music-hall licences,[20] which closed the promenades once and for all: 'No part of the house … shall habitually be used by prostitutes for the purposes of solicitation or otherwise exercising their calling.' (*The Times* 30 October 1916)

As Marie had grown older, her self-confidence had weakened. Before the Monday band call, she could not sit still. Only when the songs were rehearsed, could she face the week. Marie herself found her nerves perplexing. In an interview in 1916, she looked back to the start of her career:

I had no nerves in those days. I did not know what fear was. I was stage-struck certainly, but stage-fright I did not know. Now, I am ill a week before I sing a new song. I used to be able to sing three new songs in one evening without a shiver. But now it takes me days and days to pluck up courage to sing one. It is one of those things not easily explained. When I used to produce new songs, I argued with myself: 'Suppose I forget it and break down? Well,' I would answer, 'Suppose I do. They can't kill me.' Nowadays, I get the idea that they can kill me if I break down and so, a new song gets so much on my nerves when I am studying it, that at length I go on and sing it out of sheer desperation just to get it over. (*Newcastle Weekly Chronicle* 26 August 1916)

But in the summer of 1916, Marie's nervous health could not be blamed just on stage fright. Years of overwork, coupled with an unhappy marriage, were wearing her out. While appearing at the London Palladium with Wilkie Bard and Fred Emney, she suffered what was described as a serious nervous breakdown. For a time, it looked as though she was going the same way as Dan Leno. Her condition was termed 'very grave'. But, after a week or so, she was pronounced out of danger and on the road to recovery. In truth, though, Marie's health *was* breaking down.

Music hall, too, was under threat. The cinema was becoming more and more popular. The new music craze was ragtime. And revue was now really gaining a grip. Since it involved a company of entertainers working together in sketches and songs, it meant less work for the single turn.

In any case, the music-hall scene in London was changing dramatically. Since the start of Marie's career, the West End halls had, one by one, turned to other things: in 1894, the Trocadero closed; the Empire had started admitting revues in 1905; Sadlers Wells closed in 1906; revue took over at the Alhambra in 1912 and the Palace followed suit in 1914, the same year in which the Tivoli was closed and demolished. The Oxford, where Marie scored one of her earliest triumphs, kept going. But, if Marie needed a stark reminder about changing fashions, she got one in August 1917. She had been booked to appear at the Oxford, but was cancelled in favour of C.B. Cochran's highly popular revue, *The Better 'Ole*. Marie remained optimistic. To her, revue was just a flash in the pan – as transient as diabolo, a game which enjoyed a brief vogue:

I shouldn't be at all surprised if revues reached the end of their tether before the war does. And that, you know, wouldn't altogether be a bad thing for the music-halls. Critics are beginning to say, it's rumoured, that, although there may be exceptions, revues, taken collectively, are just a wee bit on the brainless side. This, coupled with the fact that six out of the nine big variety houses in London are now given over to revue, must provide food for serious reflection to anyone who has the welfare of the music-hall at heart; and though the music-hall is no less popular than it was a few years ago, I don't think there can be any doubt that it has lost its standing a little as a home for wit and braininess. (*Era* 21 March 1917)

Now, music-hall was great fun, but it must have surprised many people to learn that it was also witty and brainy. Marie was just trying to protect the way in which she and her friends earned their living. The comedian, Sam Mayo, provided her with a song that allowed her to poke further fun at revue:

You've got to do this
And you've got to do that
If you want to get on in revue.
Your Maudies and Bessies
That wear pretty dresses
And a dainty little shoe
Plenty of ginger
Plenty of finger
So the Johnnies in the stalls get a view
With a smile on your face
Show a little bit of lace
If you want to get on in revue.

While Marie was doing all she could for the war effort, Dillon deserted. One night, he turned up at Oakdene, Marie's home in Golders Green, demented with drink and threatening to kill her. A policeman, who was called, found a curious domestic scene. Marie and her maid were crouching in the corner of a room, while Dillon stood over them with a soda water syphon in his hand. He then set about the policeman, punching him in the face and pushing his thumb in his eye, threatening to gouge it out. He was brought before Golders Green Police Court, charged with assault. While the case was being heard, a telegram arrived from his commanding officer, asking the police to arrest him as an absentee. Dillon gave an undertaking to abstain from drink and return to his duties as a soldier; nonetheless, he was sentenced to a month's hard labour.

Four months later, he was back in court – this time charged with hitting a waiter at the Café Royal with a bottle. He was bound over for two years.

In March, 1918, Marie lost a good friend with the death of Dick Burge. Since his release from prison, he had been running the

Blackfriars Ring, a church converted into a boxing stadium – a job his widow, Bella, took over after his death.

It was in a mood of depression over Dick's death that Marie attended a dinner held in honour of theatre and music-hall people, who had either entertained the troops or raised money for those who had suffered in the war. The actress Lena Ashwell gave an address. George Robey spoke. But Marie was not asked to say anything. The *Era* recognized it as an oversight: 'Marie's generosity for any deserving object was proverbial before the war. She has never been appealed to in vain to appear at charity matinees. And many a brother and sister artiste has cause to be grateful to her for prompt assistance in their hour of need.'

Marie was getting used to being snubbed, and it continued once the War was over. In 1919, a second Royal Command Performance was arranged. George Robey, Harry Tate, Clarice Mayne and Jimmy Tate were selected. Marie was not. But was she downhearted? Well, not much. In one new song, she took a nostalgic look not just at the Great War but at the risquée label she had had to wear for nearly thirty-five years. In 'I'm a Good Girl Now' by F.E. Cliffe, M. Marcelle and L. Silberman, Marie confessed that there was nothing under the sun that she had not done. But – 'I'm a Good Girl Now!'

She played the Palladium three times, but, apart from the Holborn Empire, her appearances were either in provincial London or well away from the capital. According to Naomi Jacob,[21] her best week in 1919 was when she was paid £520 playing the Cardiff Empire.

But, even to those seeing her for the first time, she obviously retained star quality. The comedian and pantomime dame Clarkson Rose did not get to know her until after the First World War:

> I unhesitatingly think that Marie Lloyd was the greatest variety comedienne I have ever seen ... No music-hall artist has ever endeared herself to the hearts and affections of audiences – particularly London ones – more than Marie did; what an artist she was in every way. In a smart gown, sparkling jewellery, with those attractive protruding teeth and a wink that could convey a wealth of meaning, she could charm and devastate with her talent and her sex; and then, for her next item, gone would be the fashion-plate and glamour and back she would come as a bedraggled Cockney housewife. (Rose 1964)

She had other new songs in 1919. One was the joint work of Worton David and Sam Mayo – a rather melancholy song, 'I can't Forget the Days When I Was Young':

Oh, I can't forget the days when I was young
And it don't seem so very long ago
I was happy, blithe and gay
I could drive dull care away
Oh, I can't forget the days when I was young.

Fans have always enjoyed being let in on the private grief of stars. It's helped to make cult figures out of many entertainers – particularly those who died near the height of their fame. So, Marie's fans, knowing all about the rough treatment meted out to her by Dillon, really took her to their hearts when she sang about being too old to be able to 'drive dull care away'. And yet, if Marie left them wistful with that song, she could bounce back with her other new 1919 song, 'Don't Dilly Dally on the Way' – the work of Charles Collins and Fred W. Leigh. This song and 'Oh! Mr Porter' are the two Marie Lloyd songs to have best passed the test of time:

My old man said 'Follow the van
Don't dilly-dally on the way!'
Off went the cart with the home packed in it
I walked behind with my old cock linnet
But I dillied and dallied
Dallied and dillied
Lost the van and don't know where to roam
I stopp'd on the way to have the old half-quartern
And I can't find my way home.

# Chapter 24

## 1920–21

# DIVORCE FROM DILLON

1920 mixed joy and anguish, but mostly anguish. The joy came in the way Marie's fiftieth birthday was spent. A huge crowd at the Bedford gave her a rapturous reception. She rewarded them with a speech in which she said that when she first appeared at the Old Bedford she had earned fifteen shillings a week. She had had a share of life's knocks; but Providence had been good to her. Her earnest wish was to be spared a few more years so that, in public, she could please her audiences and, in private, she could help the poor. Her plans were, in fact, far-reaching. She wanted to make a world tour of all the old halls before taking a rest. She said she thought she had earned a long rest, but not yet: 'I've got to worry about the British public a bit longer, if only for the sake of paying my income tax.' (*Stage* 19 February 1920)

Given her boundless munificence, it is hard to say how wealthy she was at this stage. Alice wrote:

> The last two working years of Marie's life were not prosperous. She always worked during the latter years on sharing contracts and I have known her draw as much as £750 in a week. But, during the depression, she sometimes did no better than £23. This depression affected her health, for she had many expenses and many calls on her always open purse. (*Lloyds Sunday News* 1922)

According to Naomi Jacob (Jacob 1936) her most profitable week in 1920 was again at the Cardiff Empire, where she took £622. But Marie was very tired, and Dillon's heavy drinking was still making him violent. By May, he was barred from Oakdene. But one night he arrived uninvited. He swore at, spat in the face of, and had a fight with Marie's father, John, now aged 72. Hendon Police Court was told that there was constant quarrelling at the house. Dillon was bound over; but the situation deteriorated still further. One night towards the end of May, he broke into Oakdene and made his way to Marie's bedroom. There, he threw some beer over her and tried to pull her out of bed. Swearing all the time, he then threw a jug of water at her.

After that, Marie became so frightened that she moved out of Oakdene and stayed with friends for at least a month. At the start of July, she phoned home to speak to her cook. To her surprise, Dillon came on the line, threatening to murder her.

The following week, Marie was granted a separation order from Dillon on the grounds of 'threats, whereby she went in terror of her life, and persistent cruelty'. (*Daily Telegraph* 13 July 1920) The hearing, which was held before Hendon Magistrates, publicized the misery Marie's life had now become. Her counsel said she was suffering hell on earth. She took the proceedings with the greatest reluctance, but it was impossible for her to live with Dillon for even one more hour. She had forgiven his assaults and unfaithfulness as much as any woman could, but she was now applying to the court for protection. His attacks had been continuing for several years. Counsel also said she had suffered 'as bad an act of cruelty that a man could commit towards a woman.' (*Daily Telegraph* 13 July 1920)

Marie's maid, Maud Wilson, testified that she had seen Dillon hit Marie on many occasions. She had also seen Marie with very bad black eyes.

From the witness box, Marie said she had been knocked about so many times since the end of the previous year that she had forgotten the number. As a result, she had had to abandon work on many occasions.

Marie's doctor, Graham Hargreaves, told the court that, during the past ten years, he had treated her for a number of conditions, mostly bruises and nervous collapse.

Dillon declined to go into the witness box. But he said Marie was as much to blame as he was. He denied some of the cruelty alleged against him. He did not want a separation. He wanted a divorce.

In granting the order, the Chairman of the magistrates said he was satisfied Dillon had used threats and that he had seriously injured Marie's health.

Given Dillon's appalling behaviour and the publicity the case attracted, Marie was a brave woman indeed to turn the whole thing into a joke once she was on stage. Harry Bedford and Terry Sullivan wrote her a new song, in which she appeared as a dishevelled old crone:

I'm a bit of a ruin that Cromwell knock'd about a bit
One that Oliver Cromwell knock'd about a bit

In the gay old days, there used to be some doings
No wonder that the poor old abbey went to ruins
Those who study hist'ry sing and shout of it
And you can bet your life there isn't a doubt of it
Outside the Oliver Cromwell last Saturday night
I was one of the ruins that Cromwell knock'd about a bit.

Dillon's cruelty was now common knowledge. Even Virginia Woolf knew:

We went to the Bedford Music Hall last night and saw Miss Marie Lloyd, a mass of corruption – long front teeth – a crapulous way of saying 'desire' and yet a born artist – scarcely able to walk, waddling, aged, unblushing. A roar of laughter went up when she talked of her marriage. She is beaten nightly by her husband. (Bell 1978)

Marie's difficulty in walking was the result of arthritis. Don Ross wrote:

Arthritis gave Marie constant pain in her legs. There were times in her later life when she needed them to be massaged in her dressing-room to enable her to do her work. She would walk with slight difficulty as she made her entrance on stage. It was enough for some people in the audience to comment 'She's drunk'. It had been rumoured Marie had taken to the bottle. Marie's sister, Anne, who travelled with her on all engagements, told me in the last years, when her turbulent private life had overwhelmed her, Marie would demand a glass of champagne to be given to her at the side of the stage after each of her numbers. 'We used to put a splash of champagne in the glass and then fill it up with soda water' (said Anne). 'She'd drink it quickly and never realised it was not all champagne. She never found out. If she had, she would have murdered me.' (Ross, unpublished)

That is one story. Another was told by Walter Barfoot, a call-boy at the Finsbury Park Empire between 1915 and 1920. He said that she would normally take a drink before the first house. After the second, she was invariably the worse for wear.

Drink or no drink, it was now clear that Marie's health was breaking. In February, she was called to serve as a juror on a probate case at the Law Courts in the Strand. After an hour, the judge was told she might not be able to stand the strain of the full hearing. Looking pale, she was discharged and was helped from the jury box. Afterwards, she told a reporter that she had not been able to follow the case: 'I was much more taken up with my own pain.' (*Daily Mirror* 2 February 1921)

A few months later, Marie resolved her own probate matters. She drew up her last will, making provision for the poor of Hoxton, but leaving nothing to Dillon. In an attempt to shrug off ill health, she planned a busy year, but kept her family close by. On several bills in London, her daughter, Marie Courtenay, appeared, as well as Will Poluski, who had teamed up in a double act with Joe Mott, the son-in-law of Marie's brother, Johnny.

The most curious event of the year came in July. Despite the efforts by the theatrical hierarchs to keep Marie from appearing before royalty, she saw them off by entertaining two future kings at one go. While she was appearing at the Hippodrome, Brighton, George V's groom-in-waiting, Sir Sidney Greville, was entertaining the Duke of York (later George VI) and the Prince of Wales (later Edward VIII) at his home, the Manor House, Hove. On 18 July, he took them both to the Hippodrome. The *Brighton Gazette* carried this report:

> His [the Prince of Wales'] evident pleasure in the performance was evinced all through the programme, Miss Marie Lloyd coming in for special approval. At some of her sallies, the party rocked with laughter. Though it used not to be considered de rigueur for Royalties to applaud in theatres, our democratic Prince has set the fashion by shewing his approval in the usual way to the natural delight of the artists.

So, late in her career, Marie had conquered the Establishment.

# Chapter 25

## 1922

# FINAL PERFORMANCE

At the turn of the year, Marie was ill again. She also had an unpleasant reminder of the stresses of overworking. Clarice Mayne pulled out of the highly successful London Hippodrome pantomime, *Jack and the Beanstalk*, for which her husband, Jimmy Tate, had composed the music. Jimmy had died, a few years younger than Marie.

Nonetheless, she still travelled up and down the country – the Leeds Empire one week; the New Cross Empire in London the next; the Wolverhampton Hippodrome the week after that. At the end of March, though, her failing health again caught up with her. She was back at the Cardiff Empire, where once she had been so popular. This time, there was only a handful of people in the audience. After singing only one song, she broke down onstage and wept. She was, in any case, appearing there against doctors' advice.

However, in May, she was at the Birmingham Empire, where a reviewer for the *Encore* wrote that at her 'bright presence, darkness flies away'. In June, at the Kilburn Empire, the *Encore* said she was 'at the top of her form'; and, at the Hammersmith Palace in August, she was 'still our leading comedienne'.

The following week, she was at the Ilford Hippodrome, sharing the bill with a young comedienne, Florence Desmond: 'I knew then that she was ill, but I never dreamed that she was a dying woman. Every night I used to watch her act from the side of the stage ... Unfortunately, I never saw Marie in her prime. To me, she was a pathetic old woman, trying to carry on when she was tired and ill.' (Desmond 1953)

From Ilford, Marie went to the Alhambra. One night, she sang three or four songs, including 'Woman's Opinion of Man' and 'One of the Ruins'. But the audience were still shouting for more. Among them was J.B. Booth:

> The curtains parted and a tiny fair-haired figure – the fair hair a little tousled – in a pale rose-coloured wrap stood before the footlights. Confidentially, reminiscently, she told the stilled theatre of her early days at the Alhambra – how she had sung a song 'which wasn't rude' called 'Oh, Mr Porter'. She paused for a moment: 'Sing it with me' she pleaded and we sang:
>
> > Oh Mr Porter, what shall I do
> > I want to go to Birmingham, they've put me out at Crewe
> > Oh take me back to London as quickly as you can!
> > Oh Mr Porter, what a silly girl I am.
>
> And the man in the stall next to mine, a hard-bitten racing man, sang the words under his breath – with tears in his eyes. Was it premonition? I wonder. A sense of farewell? He was not the only one in the great theatre who felt it. I know that I did. (Booth 1943)

For the next month, Marie played halls round London, including the Putney Hippodrome, where, according to the *Encore*, she met with 'her usual reception'. The following week, she topped the bill at the Edmonton Empire. But after the first house on the Tuesday, she felt unwell. In her dressing-room, she complained of internal pains. A doctor was sent for. He suggested she went home, but she refused. She insisted she would feel better in a few moments. She intended to play the second house, as she did not want to disappoint her public. She was just like one of the lines in 'I'm a Good Girl Now': I'll carry on till I get carried off. At the second house, the booking manager for the Edmonton Empire, Leon Pollack, watched her go on:

> She was magnificent and, amid tremendous enthusiasm, she sang 'The Cosmopolitan Girl' and 'I'm one of the Ruins that Cromwell knocked about a Bit'. Never have I heard her render the songs with greater effect, but I am certain that she had not the slightest idea of what she was doing. It was purely instinct. The words and gestures, which she knew so well, came without effort. During the last few lines of 'I'm one of the Ruins', she swayed to and fro. It was the unsteadiness of a woman very, very ill. (*Performer* 11 October 1922)

As the curtain fell, she collapsed in the wings. At home in Golders Green, a specialist saw her; but he told her sisters: 'Nothing can be done for this little lady. She's dying of a broken heart.' (Anne Archer, interviewed on BBC Radio 11 February 1970)

At 11.30 p.m. that Friday, after several hours' unconsciousness, she died at the age of 52 in Rosie's arms. There were tears on her cheeks.

The next morning, the newsboys were shouting 'Marie Lloyd Dead'. People read the reports in disbelief. The bars of some pubs were wreathed in black. James Agate wrote: '[Talk of] Marie ... was in everybody's mouth that day, in club and barrack room, in bar-parlour and modest home ... Returning from Kempton, a party of bookmakers fell to speaking of the dead artist. One said ... "She had a heart, had Marie". "The size of Waterloo Station," another rejoined.' (Agate 1945)

Her brother, Johnnie, reckoned that, throughout her career, she had earned about a quarter of a million pounds, but had given most of it away.

At the funeral, at least 50,000 people lined the route from Oakdene to St Luke's Church, Hampstead, and then to Fortune Green cemetery in Hampstead. Among the mourners were song writers, taxi drivers, jockeys, entertainers, flower sellers – all sorts. One woman had even walked from Newmarket to be there.

T.S. Eliot wrote:

Marie Lloyd was the greatest music-hall artist of her time in England: she was also the most popular ... Whereas other comedians amuse their audiences as much and sometimes more than Marie Lloyd, no other comedian succeeded so well in giving expression to the life of that audience, in raising it to a kind of art. It was, I think, this capacity for expressing the soul of the people that made Marie Lloyd unique and that made her audiences, even when they joined in the chorus, not so much hilarious as happy. (Eliot 1951)

There were many tributes. Most talked of her generosity. Many said there would never be another like her. At the time, no one realized that, with her death, music-hall died, too.

Appendix I

# MARIE LLOYD'S SONGWRITERS

Some people remember the stars, others the theatres. But scarcely anyone remembers the song-writers. There were only a few of them, but between them, they wrote the songs that were not only sung then, but are still being sung now. And none of the writers became rich!

**George Arthurs** (1875–1944) began life as an accountant. For Marie, he collaborated with Fred W. Leigh on 'A Little of What You Fancy Does You Good' and with Worton David on 'The Piccadilly Trot'. He also wrote Wilkie Bard's most famous song, 'I Want to Sing in Opera', and Clarice Mayne's 'Joshua'.

**Edgar Bateman** (1860–1946) wrote the lyrics of 'Folkestone for the Day'. But his best-known songs are 'It's a Great Big Shame' and 'If It Wasn't for the Houses in Between', sung by Gus Elen. He first worked as a compositor, but later joined the publishers Francis Day and Hunter, touring the halls each night in search of new material.

**Harry Castling** (1865–1933) wrote the lyrics of 'No, 'Arry, Don't Ask Me to Marry'. His three greatest successes were Marie Kendall's theme song, 'Just Like the Ivy'; 'Let's All Go Down the Strand', sung by Charles R. Whittle, and Lily Morris's 'Don't Have Any More, Mrs Moore'.

**Fred Cliffe** (1885–1957) collaborated on 'Every Little Movement (Has A Meaning Of Its Own)' and 'I'm a Good Girl Now'. But the large part of his output was for George Formby. Three of the many songs he helped to write for Formby were 'When I'm Cleaning Windows', 'Mr Wu's a Window Cleaner Now' and 'With My Little Stick of Blackpool Rock'.

**Charles Collins** (1874–1923) collaborated on 'Don't Dilly Dally on the Way' and 'Now You've Got Your Khaki On'. He also had a hand in Harry Champion's most popular numbers, 'Any Old Iron' and 'Boiled Beef and Carrots'.

**Tom Costello** (1863–1943) wrote the melody of 'Madame Du Van'. But his writing was only a sideline; his main career was as a comedian, whose two most-liked songs were 'Comrades', written by Felix McGlennon, and 'At Trinity Church I Met My Doom', by Fred Gilbert.

(Ernest) **Worton David** (1874–1940) collaborated on 'I Can't Forget the Days When I Was Young' and 'The Piccadilly Trot'. Early in his career, he worked as a cartoonist on the *Leeds Mercury*. Through the paper, he met many entertainers appearing in Leeds and began writing songs for them. In about 1900, he moved to London and later joined the Lawrence Wright Music Company. His two biggest music-hall successes were 'Hello, Hello, Who's Your Lady Friend?' on which he collaborated with Harry Fragson, who also sang it, and Bert Lee; and Florrie Forde's 'Hold Your Hand Out, You Naughty Boy', on which he worked with C.W. Murphy.

**John P. Harrington** (1865–1939) was Marie's favourite lyricist. During his teenage years, he worked for Joe Tabrar. At the age of 19, he began a 21-year-old association with George le Brunn. After le Brunn's death, he worked with James W. Tate. Harrington reckoned that about 1,000 of his songs were published.

**George le Brunn** (1862–1905) wrote the music for Marie's first success, 'Wink the Other Eye', and continued writing for her right up to his death, mostly with John P. Harrington. When le Brunn first met Harrington, he had just finished working as a pianist at Harwood's Varieties, Hoxton. He teamed up first with Harry Adams, but, as they were, according to Harrington, 'temperamentally unsuited' (*Era* 12 October 1922), he joined forces with Harrington. It was a wonderfully productive association. Besides Marie, Harrington and le Brunn wrote for Vesta Tilley, Alec Hurley and, for a time, Charles Chaplin, father of Charlie Chaplin.

**Fred W. Leigh** (1870–1924) worked on 'Don't Dilly Dally on the Way', 'A Little of What You Fancy' and a number of other Marie Lloyd songs. His career began when he joined Francis Day and Hunter in about 1900. He was eventually appointed the firm's literary editor – a job he held until his death. Two of his most successful songs were Vesta Tilley's 'Jolly Good Luck to the Girl Who Loves A Soldier' and Vesta Victoria's 'Waiting at the Church'.

**Sam Mayo** (1881–1938) wrote the Lyrics of 'I Can't Forget the Days When I Was Young'. Mayo was both comedian and writer. On stage, he was billed as The Immobile One, singing songs to his own piano accompaniment without moving an eyelid. He was also known as a great gambler.

**A.J.** (Arthur James) **Mills** (1871–1919) was responsible for the lyrics of several Marie Lloyd songs, including 'When I Take My Morning Promenade'. His best-known songs were written in collaboration with Bennett Scott – 'Ship Ahoy! or All the Nice Girls Love a Sailor' for Hetty King, and 'Fall in and Follow Me' for Charles R. Whittle.

**Richard Morton** ( –1921) wrote the lyrics of 'Twiggy Voo', 'Don't Laugh' and 'Poor Thing'. His greatest claim to fame was as the writer of 'Ta-Ra-Ra-Boom-de-ay'. (Although, the chorus merely repeats the title word again and again, the verses are rather more complex.) Morton also worked as a dramatic critic.

**Wal Pink** ( –1922) wrote the lyrics of 'Chance Your Luck'. He began life as a comic singer, making his first public appearance at the Metropolitan in about 1886. But from 1907, he devoted himself to sketch- and lyric-writing for others. He was one of the founders of the Variety Artistes Federation and a member of the committee responsible for staging the first Royal Command Performance in 1912.

**E.W.** (Edward William) **Rogers** (1863–1913) wrote 'The Barmaid' and 'Garn Away' for Marie. In his early years, he was on the stage himself in sketches written by Harry Pleon. He chose to keep secret his song-writing, which he appears to have started towards the end of the 1880s. In collaboration with A.E. Durandeau he wrote 'Ask A Policeman' for James Fawn. He was also responsible for Vesta Tilley's 'Following in Father's Footsteps'.

**Bennett Scott** (1875–1930) wrote the music for 'When I Take My Morning Promenade' and a number of other Marie Lloyd songs. Scott began his working life in a warehouse in the City of London, but, having written songs for Vesta Victoria, Marie Kendall, Katie Lawrence and others, he had become an established writer by the autumn of 1906 when, with A.J. Mills, he founded the Star Music Publishing Company, eventually taken over by Feldman. Scott was also one of the founders of the Performing Right Society.

**Joe Tabrar** (1857–1931) was one of the most striking figures among music-hall song-writers. He was not the most modest of men, comparing himself favourably to both Wagner and Sir Arthur Sullivan. As a boy, he sang in a madrigal choir at Evans Supper Rooms. Later, he played violin in theatre pit orchestras, although he tried his hand at practically every branch of show business – clown, 'nigger minstrel', even acrobat. For Marie, he wrote the lyrics of 'Madame du Van' and 'Maid of London Ere We Part'. His biggest hit was Vesta Victoria's 'Daddy Wouldn't Buy Me A Bow-Wow', which he reckoned earned him £8.

**Howard Talbot** (1865–1928) helped to write 'Everybody Wondered How He Knew'. Talbot's real name was Munkittrick. He was born in New York, but moved to England as a child. At the Royal College of Music he studied composition under Sir Hubert Parry. He only dabbled in music-hall; musical comedy was his forte. He wrote the music of 'A Chinese Honeymoon', which had a long run at the Strand Theatre, and collaborated on 'The Arcadians' with Lionel Monckton.

**James W. Tate** (1875–1922) was intended for the Church, but he chose show business instead. He wrote the music of 'Customs of the Country' and 'My Actor Man' for Marie. Together with John P.

Harrington, he formed the Monte Carlo Publishing Company. One of Tate's greatest song-writing successes was 'If I Should Plant a Tiny Seed of Love'. He appeared on stage as accompanist to his second wife, Clarice Mayne – the couple billed as Clarice Mayne and That. For her, he wrote 'I Was a Good Little Girl (Till I Met You)'.

# MARIE LLOYD'S THEATRES

Marie played about 150 theatres in Great Britain. Here are some notes about most of them. They have nearly all gone now, most having been destroyed in the 1960s.

## Aldershot
*Hippodrome*

A collection of derelict buildings put up in the 1850s were demolished to make way for the Aldershot Hippodrome, which opened in 1913. It was still operating as a music-hall in 1957, but was pulled down in 1962.

## Bath
*Palace*

The Palace Theatre opened as the Pavilion, but was renamed the Lyric in 1895. From the earliest days, the citizens of Bath were told to behave themselves there. A programme note in 1901 informed audiences that 'the slightest attempt at disorderly conduct will be instantly and effectually suppressed'. The Lyric became the Palace in 1903. It closed as a theatre in 1955, reopening as a ballroom the following year. It is now a bingo hall.

## Belfast
*Empire*

The Belfast Empire had many forerunners. The Imperial Colosseum was built on the same site in the 1860s. This became Travers' Musical Lounge, then the New Colosseum, the Select Musical Lounge, then the Buffalo, which was rebuilt as the Empire in 1894. It was demolished in about 1961.

## Birkenhead
*Argyle*

The main claim to fame of the Argyle, which opened in 1868, was that, in 1898, Harry Lauder, then a virtual unknown, signed a contract stipulating that he would appear there every year from then on for £4 a week. Lauder kept the promise, even though not many years elapsed before he was earning many times that sum. In September 1940, the last turn one evening was Billy Scott-Comber singing 'There'll always be an England'. That night, enemy bombers scored a direct hit, burning the Argyle to the ground. What remained was demolished in 1969.

## Birmingham
*Day's Concert Hall/Empire*

Marie first appeared in Birmingham in 1887 at the Crystal Palace, later known as Day's Concert Hall, founded by James Day. In 1893, the hall was bought by Edward Moss, who engaged the greatest of all theatre architects, Frank Matcham, to redesign it. Advertised as 'the most beautiful variety theatre in England', it was re-opened as the Birmingham Empire in 1894. During an air raid in October 1940, it was bombed. It never re-opened, its remains being demolished in 1950.

*Gaiety*

'Proper' dress was the order of the day at the Gaiety. Men had to wear top hats to get in. In its early days, the Gaiety was known as Holder's after its proprietor, Henry Holder, who opened it in 1846, making it one of the earliest provincial music-halls. In 1920, it became a cinema. It closed in 1969.

'Do you think my dress is a little bit?'

Life is just a bowl of cherries!

Marie's songs remain popular even today

'Marie Lloyd was the greatest music-hall artist of her time... It was,
I think, this capacity for expressing the soul of the people that made
Marie Lloyd unique and that made her audiences, even when they
joined in the chorus, not so much hilarious as happy.'

T. S. Eliot

## Blackpool
*Alhambra*

The Prince of Wales Theatre, which had been built in 1877, was demolished to make way for the Alhambra, which opened its doors in 1899. Affording a magnificent sight from Blackpool seafront, its name changed only four years later to the Palace. It was demolished in 1962 to make way for the somewhat less spectacular Lewis's store.

*Empire*

The Blackpool Empire opened in 1895, changing its name a few years later to the Hippodrome. For some time, it operated as the Hippodrome Cinema. It was bought by ABC Ltd in 1929 and became Blackpool's new ABC Cinema (now the Cannon) in 1962.

## Bolton
*Grand*

The odd thing about the Grand was that it originally doubled as a circus. Frank Matcham designed it so that it could be converted from theatre to circus to theatre again in a matter of hours. From its opening in 1894, it played host to many of the big stars of the next 60 years. But it eventually became a bingo hall. It was demolished in 1963.

## Boscombe
*Hippodrome*

There was a public outcry when it was suggested that the Grand Theatre, which had opened in 1895 and which had played host to, among others, Sir Henry Irving, should become a music-hall. But a music-hall it became, changing its name to the Hippodrome and re-opening in 1905. It is now a discotheque.

## Bradford
*Alhambra*

The Alhambra opened as a music-hall in 1914, but became an all-purpose theatre eight years later. In 1959 it was bought by the

Bradford Corporation and it continues as a successful theatre to this day. (Much of the Albert Finney/Tom Courtenay film *The Dresser* was shot here.)

## Empire

At the opening of the Bradford Empire in 1899, Frank Allen, of Moss Empires, made this promise: 'Nothing will be seen or heard here that will raise a blush'. The theatre was the home of music-hall until 1916 when it began staging plays instead. It was all but destroyed by fire, but, after reconstruction, it reopened in 1918 as a cinema. Unfortunately, another fire closed it for good in 1952. Afterwards, it was used as a store, which was eventually demolished.

## People's Palace

The Palace began life as the Star music-hall, which opened in 1875 underneath the Princes Theatre – a possibly unique feature of theatre design. It became the People's Palace in the 1890s. By 1938, the local council had become concerned about its safety, and it closed that year.

## Brighton
*Alhambra*

The Alhambra opened in 1888. But, in 1914, it became the Palladium Cinema, which closed in 1956. That scar on the Brighton prom, the Brighton Centre, now covers the site.

## Hippodrome

An ice rink, built in 1897, was converted by Frank Matcham into a theatre in 1900. It opened the following year as the Hippodrome and became a bingo hall in 1963. Some charming features of the theatre are still to be seen, including some intricate tiles in the doorways, depicting sea-serpents.

## Bristol
*Empire*

The Bristol Empire had three lives. As a theatre, it opened in 1893. It turned into a cinema in 1931, reverting to live shows in 1939. Finally, it became BBC studios in 1954, but was demolished in 1963.

*Hippodrome*

The Bristol Hippodrome, designed by Frank Matcham, opened in 1912. It was a rather more ornate structure than it is today, but at least it is still operating as a theatre.

## Cardiff
*Empire*

The Cardiff Empire was first known as Levino's Hall. It became the Empire Palace of Varieties in 1889, but outgrew itself. Frank Matcham designed a new Cardiff Empire, which was built in four months. It was opened in 1896 only to be destroyed by fire three years later. Matcham designed a new theatre, which was opened in 1900. It was again rebuilt and remained a variety theatre until it was converted into the Gaumont Cinema. It was demolished in 1961. Offices and shops now stand on the site.

## Chatham
*Barnard's New Palace of Varieties*

In 1851, the Granby Head pub was bought by Sam Barnard. He changed its name to the Railway Tavern and Hall of Varieties. It burned down in 1885. In 1886, it re-opened as Barnard's New Palace of Varieties, but it was destroyed by another fire in 1934. A Lyons teashop was built in its place, but even that has disappeared in this lugubrious town centre.

*Gaiety*

The Imperial Music-Hall opened behind what is now the Imperial Hotel in about 1835. In 1890, it was replaced by the Gaiety Theatre of

Varieties. Having been re-designed by Frank Matcham, it became the Chatham Empire in 1912. It closed in 1960 to make way for a car park.

## Colchester
*Grand*

This theatre opened on Easter Monday 1905. Later, it became a Hippodrome, but a fire, which destroyed the stage in 1972, put a stop to all live entertainment. For a time it was a bingo hall, but it is now a so-called entertainments centre. One good feature of the conversion is that the carved name 'Grand' can still be seen at the top of the building.

## Coventry
*Hippodrome*

The first Coventry Hippodrome was a corrugated iron hut, but this was replaced by a proper theatre, which opened on New Year's Eve 1906. In 1937, it was replaced by the third Hippodrome built right next door. During the Second World War, it was the target of scores of bombs, one of which went right through the theatre without exploding. In later years, the Hippodrome became the Apollo Theatre. It closed in 1983 to become a bingo hall.

## Derby
*Grand*

Only two months after this theatre opened in 1886, it was destroyed by fire; but it was rebuilt during the same year. It closed in 1950, later becoming a dance-hall. It is now a night club, although the original theatre façade remains.

*Hippodrome*

The Derby Hippodrome opened in 1914, but was converted into a cinema in 1930. During the Second World War it became a variety theatre again and presented live entertainment until 1959. In the early 1960s it became a bingo hall.

# Douglas, Isle of Man
*Derby Castle*

Derby Castle opened for entertainment in 1877. The Aquadrome now stands on the site.


*Pavilion*

The Pavilion opened in 1893, but was magnificently rebuilt by Frank Matcham in 1900. Now known as the Gaiety, the theatre has been splendidly refurbished in recent years under the direction of the eminent theatre architect Victor Glasstone.


# Dundee
*Kings*

The lavish decor of the Kings Theatre, which opened in 1909, remains intact, although it no longer serves as a theatre. It became a cinema in 1928 and a bingo hall in the early 1980s.


# Eastbourne
*Hippodrome*

Hurrah! This is one of the few variety theatres still going. Designed by C.J. Phipps, who was also responsible for the Savoy, Lyric and Her Majesty's theatres in London, it opened in 1883 as the Theatre Royal. It is now known as the Royal Hippodrome.


# Edinburgh
*Empire*

Edward Moss hoped that the first Royal Command Performance in 1912 would be staged at the Edinburgh Empire, which had opened in 1892. But it was destroyed in 1911 by the fire which killed the illusionist Lafayette. It was rebuilt in 1912 and again in 1928. After running at a loss of up to £1,000 a week, it closed as a theatre in 1962. Since then, it has been a bingo hall.

### Exeter
*Hippodrome*

Exeter was the home town of the comedian Fred Karno. He was the first owner of the Exeter Hippodrome, which opened in 1908 in a building dating from the early nineteenth century. It was converted into a cinema in 1931, but was destroyed by bombing in 1942.

### Folkestone
*Town Hall*

Marie visited the town she eulogized in 'Folkestone for the Day' in 1896. She appeared at the imposing Town Hall, now (incredibly) a chemists.

### Glasgow
*Coliseum*

This vast theatre, designed by Frank Matcham, used to seat about 2,700 people. It opened in 1905. It became a cinema, but it closed in 1982.

*Empire/Gaiety/Scotia*

Known throughout the profession as the comics' graveyard, the Glasgow Empire was built to Frank Matcham's design on the site of the old Gaiety Theatre. The Gaiety, in turn, had replaced the Scotia, which closed the same year as it opened – 1897. Stories about the toughness of Glasgow Empire audiences are legion. Asked if he had ever appeared there, Max Miller replied: 'I'm a comedian, not a missionary'. Des O'Connor fainted on stage. (Eric Morecambe used to add that, when Des came round and started singing, the audience fainted.) After the final performance in 1963, the Glasgow Empire was demolished.

*Pavilion*

The Glasgow Pavilion, which opened in 1904, is another of the handful of variety theatres still going.

# Great Yarmouth
*Wellington Pier Pavilion*

Nicknamed the Cowshed, the Pavilion was opened in 1903 – nearly 50 years after the Pier itself was built. Over the years, it's been the home of variety shows, concert parties, even political meetings. Despite a plethora of theatres in Yarmouth, this theatre, too, is still going strong.

# Hanley
*Grand*

The people of Hanley took a severe view of some music-hall performers. In an article marking the twenty-first anniversary of the Grand, the *Staffordshire Sentinel* reported: 'Comedians, who think that suggestiveness is funny ... are sternly suppressed when discovered'. The Grand – another Frank Matcham theatre – opened in 1898. It was converted into a cinema in 1932, but was destroyed by fire three months later.

# Hastings
*Hippodrome*

Marie headed the bill that opened this theatre on Hastings seafront in 1899. It later changed its name to the Empire Palace of Varieties, then became the Cinema de Luxe, despite being known as the draughtiest theatre in town. When films became unprofitable, it became a bingo hall. By 1970, even bingo did not pay, and it is now the De Luxe Pleasure Centre, crammed with fruit machines.

# Hull
*Palace*

Built to the design of Frank Matcham, the Palace opened in 1897. It was enlarged in 1928, but became an early casualty of the Second World War. Badly damaged in an air raid, it remained closed for ten years. After being repaired, it reopened in 1951. It finally closed in 1965 and was demolished the following year.

## Ipswich
*Hippodrome*

During its eighty years, the Ipswich Hippodrome enjoyed at least four lives. It opened as a theatre, designed by Frank Matcham, in 1905, became a cinema in 1930 and reopened as a theatre in 1941. Shortly before closing as a theatre for the last time in 1957, fire broke out in the circle while Hutch was on stage, singing 'I Don't Want to Set the World on Fire'. In 1959, it became a ballroom and finally served as a bingo hall. It was demolished in 1985. An office block now marks the spot.

## Leeds
*Empire*

The Leeds Empire, which opened in 1898, was at first so successful that the city's two other music-halls, the Tivoli and the City Varieties, were forced to close for a while. Until the 1950s, top-line entertainers came here. Moss Empires planned to build a larger theatre in its place, but it never happened. The last show was *Babes in the Wood* in 1960–1. As the curtains fell for the last time, one of the pantomime's stars, Nat Jackley (a distant relative, incidentally, of Marie) stepped forward, removed his wig and explained 'You always raise your hat when you say goodbye to an old friend'. The Empire was pulled down in 1962.

*Princess Palace*

A wooden theatre, called the New, which opened in 1848, was rebuilt and renamed the Princess Concert Hall. It opened on Christmas Eve 1874. Later, it became the Tivoli, then the Hippodrome, but, by the late 1920s, audiences were dwindling. It closed in 1933, was used as a clothing workshop and warehouse for some time, and was eventually demolished in 1967.

## Leicester
*Empire*

Sam Sweeney, who had been the Chairman at the Argyle in Birkenhead, relaunched the Gaiety Palace of Varieties as the Leicester Empire in 1894. Later, the theatre became a cinema called the Hippodrome; but it closed in the late 1930s.

*Palace*

Oswald Stoll opened this theatre, designed by Frank Matcham, in 1901. It presented variety until the mid-1950s, when it closed for a while. On reopening, it staged nude shows. It finally closed in 1959 in readiness for its demolition the following year.

*Tivoli*

People with long memories in Leicester called this the 'Old Pav', because, although the theatre had started out as the Prince of Wales in 1890 and had become the Tivoli in 1896, it was the Pavilion from about the turn of the century. Its last performance was in 1930. It was pulled down to make way for wider roads.

**Liverpool**
*Empire*

The Liverpool Empire dates from 1896 when it took the place of the Alexandra Theatre, which had been built in 1867. Over the years, it has undergone drastic alterations, but it is still operating as a theatre.

*Grand*

At the end of the eighteenth century, this theatre was a chapel. It was converted in 1849 and opened the following year as the Royal Colosseum Theatre and Music-Hall. It underwent many changes of name, but became the Grand Theatre of Varieties in 1884 and, more plainly, the Grand Theatre ten years later. It was demolished and rebuilt in 1904 and took on two more names – Queen's Theatre and Kelly's Theatre – before being demolished in 1920–1.

*Olympia*

Frank Matcham, who designed the Olympia for Moss Empires in 1905, made this building nearly as large as his London masterpiece, the Coliseum. (Marie would have enjoyed the fact that it had been built on the site of the former Licensed Victuallers' Asylum.) It became a cinema in 1925, a dance hall in 1949, and is now a bingo hall.

**London**
Balham
*Duchess/Hippodrome*

This music-hall, designed by W.G.R. Sprague, opened in 1899. It eventually became the Balham Hippodrome, but it ceased operating as a theatre at the outset of the Second World War. It was demolished in the 1960s.

Bermondsey
*Star*

Originally the Star and Garter pub, this music-hall operated from 1867 until 1919. It was demolished in 1963.

Bethnal Green
*Foresters*

What was once the Artichoke pub became the Foresters in 1889. It ceased life as a theatre in 1917 and eventually became a cinema; it closed in 1960 and was demolished.

Bow
*Eastern Empire*

The Eastern Empire was first a music-hall in 1855 under the name of the Three Cups Public House and Music Hall. It became a cinema in 1923, but closed in 1958. It was then demolished.

Brixton
*Empress*

This music-hall opened at Christmas 1898. It later became the Granada Cinema. There is currently talk of it being demolished to make way for houses and offices.

Camberwell
*Metropole*

It was the Metropole when it opened in 1894, but it became the Camberwell Empire in 1906. It was pulled down to make way for wider roads in 1937.

*Palace*

The Camberwell Palace opened in 1899. It eventually became a cinema, but closed in the mid-1950s.

Camden Town
*Bedford*

The history of this music-hall goes back to about 1824 when it was known as the Bedford Arms Tavern and Teas Garden. Its name changed to the Bedford Music-Hall and it alternated between that and the Bedford Palace of Varieties until 1941. It closed during the 1950s and was demolished in 1969.

Central London
*Alhambra*

Six years after its opening as the grandly titled Panoptican of Science and Art, this theatre, situated in Leicester Square, became a music-hall in 1860. Leotard, the original daring young man on the flying trapeze, was one of the first entertainers to appear here. Ballet once formed part of the entertainment there, but the magistrates at the Middlesex Sessions refused the theatre a music and dancing licence on account of indecency: the can-can had been danced there! A series of promenade concerts was then arranged, but these were also deemed to infringe licensing regulations. The theatre was forced to close at the beginning of 1871, but for only four months. It was destroyed by fire in 1882. Another Alhambra was put up, but it was demolished in 1937 to make way for the Odeon Cinema.

*Charing Cross*

Now better known as the Players Theatre, this is at present being reconstructed as part of a large redevelopment programme between Charing Cross station and the Thames. The theatre opened as The Arches in 1867.

*Empire*

There has been entertainment on the site of the Empire Theatre, Leicester Square, since 1849. The Empire opened in 1884. It continued presenting live entertainment until 1927, the last show being Gershwin's *Lady Be Good* –a possible epitaph for the ladies who had caused such controversy in the promenade. The theatre was demolished to make way for the Empire cinema.

*London Pavilion*

The London Pavilion stood originally in Tichborne Street. It was demolished in 1885 and a new theatre built in Piccadilly. It was converted into a cinema in 1934 and to a shopping arcade recently.

*Middlesex*

The roots of the Middlesex, Drury Lane, were in the seventeenth century. What at one time was the Mogul music-hall became the Middlesex in 1851 and the Winter Garden in 1919. The theatre closed in 1959 to be redeveloped as the New London Theatre in 1971–2.

*Oxford*

London's first purpose-built music-hall opened under the aegis of Charles Morton in 1891. But, by 1913, touring revues and musical comedies were being staged there. It was closed in 1920 to be converted into a theatre proper. But the new theatre closed in 1926 and was later demolished.

## Palace

The Palace was first an opera house. It opened in 1891, but quickly failed and became a variety theatre in 1892. Since then, it has been the home of many successful musicals.

## Palladium

Possibly the most famous variety theatre in the world, the Palladium was built to Frank Matcham's design, and opened in 1910. And [again hurrah!] it's still going strong.

## Royal, Holborn

Weston's music-hall opened on this site in 1857. Eleven years later, it became the Royal and eventually the Holborn Empire, the home of Max Miller and Gracie Fields. It was destroyed by enemy bombing in 1940.

## Theatre Royal

One of the most historic theatres in London, the first theatre opened in Drury Lane in 1732. It was the size of the stage of the present theatre.

## Tivoli

The Tivoli, which stood in the Strand, opened in 1890. It lasted until only 1914, when it was demolished. The site remained vacant until 1923 when a cinema was built.

## Trocadero

Originally the Royal Albion Theatre in Great Windmill Street, this became the Royal Trocadero Palace of Varieties in 1882. Albert Chevalier and Hugh Jay Didcott took over in 1893, but their company went bankrupt and the theatre closed. In 1902, it was converted into a restaurant, where entertainment was staged.

Chelsea
*Palace*

Chelsea's music-hall had a life of just over fifty years. It opened in 1903 and was converted into a studio for Granada Television in 1957. It remained so until 1965 and was demolished the following year.

Chiswick
*Empire*

The Chiswick Empire had more than a touch of drama. Even before it was built, many local people complained that it would lower the tone of the area. It was built, but, within a year, fire destroyed the stage and damaged the auditorium. While repairs were being carried out, the theatre was closed for a few months. During the height of the bombing of the Second World War, it closed again. Then, two years after the war, part of the ceiling collapsed, injuring some of the audience. In between times, the shows went on, the last one in 1959 starring Liberace. The theatre was demolished the following year to make way for offices.

Clapham
*Grand*

The Grand was opened in 1900. It eventually became a cinema and, then, a bingo hall. At the moment, it stands empty.

Crouch End
*Hippodrome*

Originally the Queens Opera House, this theatre opened in 1897. It was damaged by enemy bombs in 1942 and never reopened.

Croydon
*Hippodrome*

The Hippodrome opened as the Empire Theatre of Varieties in 1898, but became the Hippodrome in 1911. It closed in 1956, the site being used for an extension for British Home Stores.

*Palace*

This theatre, built in 1895, opened as the New National Hall and Grand Circus. After being rebuilt, it reopened in 1906 as the Empire Palace. In 1930, it became the Empire Cinema, but reopened as a music-hall in 1938. It became the Eros cinema in 1953, but closed in 1959. It has since been demolished.

Ealing
*Hippodrome*

The Hippodrome was just one of the names conferred on this splendidly ornate theatre. It began life in the 1880s as the Lyric Hall and was later called the Hippodrome, the Ealing Theatre and the Broadway Cinema before it ended up as the Palladium Cinema. The demolition men moved in in 1958. A branch of W.H. Smith's now graces the site.

East Ham
*Palace*

This music-hall lasted just over half a century. It was built in 1906 and closed in 1957. It was demolished the following year.

Edmonton
*Empire*

Renowned as being the theatre where Marie gave her last performance, the Edmonton Empire opened in 1908. It was converted into a cinema in 1933. In 1951, its name was changed to the Granada. All-in wrestling matches were staged during the 1960s. It closed in 1968 and was demolished two years later. Part of the brickwork of the foundations can now be seen in a shopping centre car park.

Euston
*Varieties*

The Euston Varieties became the Regent Theatre in 1900. From the early 1930s, it was used as a cinema.

Finsbury Park
*Empire*

Another Frank Matcham theatre, the Finsbury Park empire opened in 1910. It closed in 1960 and was demolished in 1965.

Fulham
*Granville*

A magnificent Matcham theatre, the Granville opened its doors in 1898. Towards the end of its life, it was an industrial film studio. Its demolition in 1971 was a scandal.

Golders Green
*Hippodrome*

Towards the end of her life, this was Marie's local theatre. Designed by Bertie Crewe (with one box facing the audience, rather than the stage), it opened on Boxing Day 1913. As a theatre, the last show to be staged there was *Sleeping Beauty* with Danny La Rue. It closed in 1968 and could have been demolished for redevelopment. But it was saved by the BBC, which now uses it for radio shows such as *Friday Night is Music Night*.

Hackney
*Empire*

Despite many difficulties, the splendid Hackney Empire is still presenting variety shows, thanks to the hard work of its Preservation Trust. Built in 1901, to Frank Matcham's design, it played host to scores of big names. In the late 1950s, it became a television studio and a few years after that a bingo hall. It returned to its roots in 1986. Long may it prosper!

*Sebright*

The Sebright music-hall, sometimes known as English's Sebright, opened in 1865. But it lost some of its prestige once the Empire opened. It became the Regent Theatre of Varieties, which showed films, as well as staging variety turns. It was demolished in 1938. A block of flats now marks the spot.

## Hammersmith
*Palace of Varieties*

The Hammersmith Centre now stands on the site of this old theatre, which operated as a music-hall from 1880. It was rebuilt in 1898 and underwent further alterations under Frank Matcham's guidance in 1910.

## Holloway
*Empire*

The Holloway Empire, designed by W.G.R. Sprague, opened in 1899. But, by the mid-1920s, it had become a cinema. It was sold in 1953 and demolished in the mid-1970s.

## Hoxton
*Varieties*

The Hoxton Varieties, known locally as the Flea-pit, opened in 1870. Later that year, George Harwood took over. At each performance, he stood at the pit entrance collecting the twopenny entrance fees in a bookmaker's satchel. At the end of a week, his entertainers were paid in coins of all denominations. Gus Leach succeeded him as licensee; and later, G.H. Macdermott took charge. The theatre eventually became a cinema, but was demolished in 1981.

## Ilford
*Hippodrome*

The Ilford Hippodrome, designed by Frank Matcham, opened in 1909. During the performance of a pantomime in 1945, enemy action demolished the dressing rooms and part of the auditorium, causing scenery to crash down on the stage and showering the audience with dust and debris. Amazingly, no one was killed. Two days later, the roof collapsed. After the theatre had stood empty for more than a decade, the local council ordered its demolition in 1957.

Islington
*Collins*

In this most famous music-hall, many people claim to have seen ghosts. Marie is once said to have sworn she saw an old Irishman appear in her dressing-room, grin affably and walk through the wall. Formerly a pub, it became Collins in 1863 when Sam Vagg, a chimney sweep, took it over. Calling himself Sam Collins, he alternated between serving behind the bar and singing the customers Irish ballads. He enlarged and redecorated the pub, but, within three years, he had died at the age of 39. It remained Collins for nearly a century. After being badly damaged by fire in 1958, it never reopened.

*Grand/Empire*

There were, in all, four theatres on this site. It opened as the Philharmonic Hall in 1860. It became the Philharmonic Theatre, the Grand Theatre and finally the Islington Empire. The last variety show was staged in 1932. The Empire became a cinema and was demolished in the early 1960s.

Kilburn
*Empire*

Built in 1899, the Kilburn Empire was designed to be both music-hall and a circus. It became a full-time cinema in 1928 and remained virtually unchanged until 1971 when it was largely rebuilt. But from its circus days, rare elephant pits are still to be seen beneath the stage. Its last name was the Broadway. Now boarded up, it presents a sorry sight.

Kings Cross
*Palace, Euston*

This music-hall, which opened on Boxing Day, 1900, eventually became the Regent Theatre. From about 1932, it was used as a cinema.

Kingston upon Thames
*Empire*

The upper part of this Edwardian theatre can still be seen – with weeds growing out of the roof. At ground level, there are modern shops, but above them the name 'Empire' can still be seen, together with the date the theatre opened – 1910. Variety shows were staged there until the 1950s. The theatre closed in 1955.

Lambeth
*Canterbury*

This famous music-hall started out as a pub – the Canterbury Arms. A small hall was built in 1852, replaced by a larger one in 1854 and rebuilt in 1876. It was remodelled by Frank Matcham in 1890. Enemy action caused extensive damage in 1942 and what was left of the Canterbury was demolished in the 1950s.

*South London*

The first South London Palace of Varieties, which opened in 1860, was destroyed by fire in 1869. Another music-hall was built. This lasted until the Second World War, when it was damaged by enemy bombs. It was demolished in 1955.

*Surrey*

This music-hall had a long history: there were successively three theatres in all. The first, which opened in 1782 as the Royal Circus, was burnt down, as was the second. The third was converted into a music-hall in 1904. At the start of the 1920s, it was a cinema. It was demolished in 1934. The site was bought by the Royal Eye Hospital.

Lewisham
*Hippodrome*

This landmark – the work of Frank Matcham – lasted 50 years. It was opened in 1911 and was demolished in 1961.

New Cross
*Empire*

This Frank Matcham theatre opened in 1899. It continued staging variety shows until the early 1950s. It closed in 1954 and was demolished in 1956. A petrol station now stands on the site.

Paddington
*Metropolitan*

The demolition of this beautiful music-hall represents another major London planning scandal. It closed at the end of 1962 and was pulled down to make way for a motorway. In the event, the motorway took a different route, and so the Met need never have gone. It had been built on the site of a sixteenth-century inn. As a theatre, it harked back to the 1860s. It was rebuilt in 1897 to the design of Frank Matcham and contained some of his most ornate and inventive work.

Peckham
*Crown*

The Crown opened as the Peckham Hippodrome in 1898. It became the Gaumont cinema, but closed in 1961.

Penge
*Empire*

Designed by W.G.R. Sprague, this theatre opened as the New Empire in 1915. In 1949, it became the Essoldo cinema. The last film was shown in 1960, and the building was pulled down later that year.

Poplar
*Hippodrome*

The Poplar Hippodrome opened at Christmas 1905. It became a cinema 20 years later, but was virtually destroyed in the Second World War. It was demolished in 1950.

*Queens*

This theatre lasted 100 years. It was first licensed as a music-hall in 1856, and closed in 1956.

Putney
*Hippodrome*

This music-hall opened in 1906. It became a cinema in the 1930s. The last film was shown in 1961, and the building was demolished in 1975 to make way for houses.

Shepherd's Bush
*Empire*

Another Frank Matcham theatre, the Shepherd's Bush Empire opened in 1903 and closed almost exactly 50 years later. BBC Television have been running it since.

Shoreditch
*Eagle*

This music-hall, where Marie made her debut, deserves a book to itself. The Eagle, featured in the rhyme, 'Pop Goes The Weasel', stood next to the illustrious Grecian Theatre. It appears to have closed in 1887.

*Falstaff*

This was another music-hall at which Marie appeared early in her career. Its life spanned the second half of the nineteenth century.

*London*

Better known later as the Shoreditch Empire, this music-hall began life in 1856 as the Griffin. It was bought by a drapery warehouse company in 1934 and was demolished the following year.

*Royal Cambridge*

The original Cambridge, which opened in 1864, was destroyed by fire in 1896. The second building was demolished in 1936 to make way for the extension of a tobacco factory.

*Standard/Olympia*

There was entertainment here from as early as 1837 when the premises were known as the Royal Standard Public House and Pleasure Gardens. It appears to have ceased operating as a theatre in 1926. It was demolished in 1940.

Stepney
*Paragon*

This well-known East End music-hall was also designed by Frank Matcham. It took the place of the infamous Lusby's. It was opened in 1885 and changed its name to the Mile End Empire in 1912. It was demolished to make way for a cinema in 1937.

Stoke Newington
*Palace*

Designed by Frank Matcham, this music-hall opened as the New Alexandra Theatre in 1897. After the Second World War, it was used for a variety of purposes, but it closed in 1950.

Stratford
*Borough*

Another Frank Matcham theatre, the Borough was opened in 1896. In 1933, it became a cinema, and it ended up as a bingo hall.

*Empire*

One of the most famous music-halls in East London, the Stratford Empire opened in 1899. As a young boy, Stanley Holloway watched

Marie here. The Empire was hit by a bomb in 1940 and remained derelict until it was demolished in 1958.

## Tottenham
*Palace*

This theatre opened in 1908. Films were shown between 1924 and 1926, when it became a theatre again. It closed in 1969 and is now a bingo hall.

## Walthamstow
*Palace*

'Aunt Alice' was the local rhyming slang for this theatre, whose twin towers were a feature of Walthamstow for nearly 60 years. It opened just after Christmas 1903. After music-hall's heyday, it tried everything: revues, dance bands, even nude shows. It finally turned to plays, but the last was performed in 1954. After its demolition in 1960, a parade of shops was built on the site.

## Willesden
*Hippodrome*

Although this theatre was known as the Willesden Hippodrome, it stood, in fact, in Harlesden. It, too, was designed by Frank Matcham. Having opened in 1907, its life was effectively ended in 1940 when a high-explosive bomb destroyed the stage and a large part of the back. Another seventeen years elapsed before it was demolished to be replaced by characteristically drab government offices.

## Wood Green
*Empire*

Yet another plush Frank Matcham creation in cream and gold with red seating, this opened in 1912. In 1912, the illusionist Chung Ling Soo (real name, William Robinson) was killed on stage when a trick misfired. After a production of *Cinderella*, starring Monsewer Eddie Gray and Arthur English, the Wood Green Empire closed in 1955. It was later demolished.

Woolwich
*Barnards*

Barnard's music-hall in Woolwich opened in 1834 as the New Portable Theatre. It eventually became the Woolwich Empire. Towards the end of its life, it staged strip shows. Its last – in 1958 – was called *Ecstasie*. It was demolished in 1960.

*Hippodrome*

The Woolwich Hippodrome opened in 1900, but became a cinema in 1924.

**Manchester**
*Ardwick Empire*

'Empire at Ardwick Green: Always Ask For The Tram Junction': so ran the advertisements proclaiming this theatre, which opened in 1904. In 1935, it was renamed the New Manchester Hippodrome. After its closure in 1961, it was demolished.

*Folly/Tivoli*

A Methodist chapel, built in the 1830s, was converted into the Alexandra music-hall in 1865. It became the Folly in 1879 and the Tivoli in 1897. It closed in 1921.

*Palace*

The Palace, which opened in 1891, was played by most leading music-hall and variety entertainers. It closed in 1978, but was then bought from Moss Empires. A trust was formed and, after restoration costing £3 million, the Palace reopened in 1981.

**Mansfield**
*Empire*

The Mansfield Empire opened a few days before the outbreak of the First

World War. It became a cinema before closing in 1960. In latter years, it was used as a warehouse before being demolished to make way for a ring road in 1981.

## Margate
*Hippodrome*

The Margate Hippodrome opened in 1898. Over the next 60 years or so, it dodged between being a theatre and a cinema, the last show being given in 1959. Seven years later, it was pulled down and Margate Library, possibly the ugliest building in the town, now stands on the site.

## Middlesbrough
*Empire*

The Middlesbrough Empire opened in 1899 with seating for 2,000 people. In 1963, it was sold to Mecca to be used as a bingo hall. But, from time to time, it still stages live shows.

## Newcastle upon Tyne
*Empire*

The Newcastle Empire opened in 1890, but was almost entirely remodelled by Frank Matcham in 1903. The theatre was sold to the local council in 1960 and was demolished to make way for a shopping centre.

*Olympia*

This theatre began life in 1893 as a corrugated iron hall. After a fire, it was rebuilt in 1908. It became a cinema, but was closed in 1960 and demolished in 1971.

## Newport
*Empire*

The Newport Empire was the fourth theatre to open on the same site, the first being the Parrot, which was built in about 1814. The Empire opened in 1899. Shows were staged there until 1942, when fire broke out. The Empire never reopened, although it was some years before it was demolished. Its place was eventually taken by a Woolworth store, but this, too, has now closed.

## Northampton
*New*

The architect W.G.R. Sprague joined civic dignitaries on stage at the opening of the New Theatre in 1912. Over the next 40 years, dozens of big names appeared here. But, by the late 1950s, it was presenting strip shows. The last was *Strip! Strip! Horray!* (the show of lovely ladies and lively lads). The New closed in 1958 and was demolished two years later. Its site is now occupied by a clothing store.

## Norwich
*Hippodrome*

Marie liked to ensure that her visits to Norwich coincided with racing at Newmarket. The Hippodrome opened in 1903 as the Grand Opera House. The architect was W.G.R. Sprague. Within a year, it had become a music-hall. It was converted into a cinema in 1930. From 1937, it alternated between being a theatre and cinema; but it closed in 1960. It was demolished in 1966.

## Nottingham
*Empire*

The Nottingham Empire, which opened in 1898, brought Edward Moss and Oswald Stoll together for the first time. Both men wanted a music-hall in the centre of Nottingham, and the Empire was designed by Frank Matcham. For nearly 60 years, it played host to practically every major name in music-hall and variety. It finally staged strip shows before it closed in 1958. It was demolished in 1969.

*Palace*

The Palace evolved from a skating rink. It became the Talbot Palace of

Varieties in 1876 and operated under a variety of names before becoming the Kings Theatre in 1902. Later, it was converted into a cinema – the Scala – and it is now a pub.

## Plymouth
*Palace Theatre of Varieties*

Disaster struck the Theatre of Varieties early in its life. Only seven months after its opening in 1898, it was badly damaged by fire. During a battle scene, pieces of burning paper flew around, eventually setting the stage alight. The theatre was closed for several months while repairs were carried out. It presented live entertainment up to the 1950s; but it was turned into a bingo hall before becoming a night club in 1984.

## Portsmouth
*Empire*

Portsmouth's Empire Theatre was designed by C.J. Phipps. It opened in 1891. After renovation in 1913, it changed its name to the Coliseum. On its reopening, Marie topped the bill. It reverted to its old title in 1950, but for only a few years. It was demolished in 1958. A supermarket now stands on the site.

*Hippodrome*

The Portsmouth Hippodrome was built in 1907, but was destroyed by enemy action in 1941.

## Reading
*Palace of Varieties*

This theatre lasted a little over 50 years. Designed by W.G.R. Sprague, it opened in 1907 and closed in 1960. It was demolished the following year to make way for an office block.

**Salford**
*Regent*

Known as the Regent Theatre or Regent Opera House, this magnificent theatre, once more the work of Frank Matcham, opened in 1895. In its early years, Houdini appeared there, and so did Grock. In 1919, it became the Palace. Ten years later, it was converted into two cinemas – the Salford Palace and the Palace Cinema. Despite showing films, the Palace did host the finals of the Salford Cotton Queen competition and the annual pantomimes of the Salford Police and Fire Brigade. In 1941, the Palace Cinema caught fire and never reopened. But the Salford Palace continued, reverting, in fact, to live variety in 1950. Fire struck again in 1952, completely destroying the inside of the building. It was demolished in 1963.

**Sheffield**
*Empire*

Another Frank Matcham theatre, the Sheffield Empire opened in 1895. Over the years, it presented variety, revues, musical comedies and plays. Frankie Howerd made his professional début here in 1946. The Empire soldiered on until 1959, when it closed. It was demolished in the same year.

**Southampton**
*Hippodrome*

On land once used for circuses in Southampton, the Prince of Wales's Royal Theatre opened in 1883. For nearly 25 years, plays were staged there. But, in 1905, it was converted into the Hippodrome. The last show was staged in 1939. The theatre was destroyed by bombing during the following year.

*Royal York/Palace*

Straw and sawdust covered the floor of the old Royal York Theatre, which opened in 1872. It was a music-hall of the old school. During the mid-1890s, it was destroyed by fire. The Palace was built in its place, opening in 1898. It was destroyed by enemy action.

## Southend
*Hippodrome*

One of the most important events in the Southend social calendar was the crowning of the Carnival Queen, which took place at the Hippodrome, built in 1909. The theatre finally succumbed to films in 1936 when it became the Gaumont cinema. It was demolished in 1958.

*Pier Pavilion*

Southend's Pier Pavilion opened in 1889. During the 1950s, the author saw a summer show there. His only memory of it is that the singing and dancing had to compete with the noise of the pier trains trundling to and fro. The theatre was badly damaged by fire in 1959 and was replaced by a bowling alley in 1962.

## Southsea
*Kings*

Yet another Frank Matcham theatre, the Kings, which opened in 1907, is still operating.

## South Shields
*Thornton's Varieties/Empire Palace*

Originally Thornton's Varieties, the Empire Palace, designed by Frank Matcham, opened in 1899. During the 1930s, it was rebuilt as a cinema. It is now a bingo club.

## Sunderland
*Empire*

Vesta Tilley declared the Sunderland Empire open in 1907. It served as a variety theatre until the 1920s; then came films, revues and touring musical comedies. By the 1950s, it was staging strip shows. But the local Council bought it in 1960 to run as a theatre – and it has gone from strength to strength ever since.

*People's Palace*

Before the Empire, the Palace was the only music-hall in Sunderland. It opened in 1891. After closing for a fortnight in 1930, it reopened as a cinema; but the last film was shown in 1956. The cinema was eventually demolished to make way for a leisure centre.

### Swansea
*Empire*

This theatre opened in 1898 as the Swansea Pavilion, but became the Empire in 1904. It was later a cinema and a bingo hall, but was demolished in 1960.

### Watford
*Palace*

On land once occupied by a pierrots' marquee, the Palace was built in 1908. Placards announced that shows would be staged 'such as to be found in the Metropolis, but without the inconvenience of an irksome railway journey' ... and so it continues to this day.

### Wolverhampton
*Hippodrome*

The Wolverhampton Hippodrome opened as the Empire Palace in 1898, changing its name in 1921. A fire destroyed the auditorium in 1956 and the theatre was demolished two years later.

### York
*Empire*

*Cinderella* starring Florrie Forde was the York Empire's first production in 1902. From then on the theatre staged opera, a Paul Raymond revue, carol concerts and wrestling. At one point, there was roller skating, at another, bingo. In 1989, after four years' restoration, it was reopened as a theatre.

# NOTES

1 Alice took the surname Lloyd in 1890. From 1890 to 1896, she appeared with the Woods' third daughter, Gracie, to form the Sisters Lloyd. They made their début at the Foresters Music-Hall in London and went on to play other halls in London and the provinces. They also appeared in pantomime in Portsmouth; the Grand, Islington, and the Pavilion, Aldgate. They considered their most successful songs to be 'Cinderella Up-to-date' and 'Quarrelling'. When Gracie married a jockey, George Hyams, in 1896, she retired from the stage. Alice continued as a solo entertainer, marrying Tom McNaughton, who, with his brother, Fred, formed the Two McNaughtons (or the Brothers McNaughton), a pair of quick-fire patter comedians, who first appeared as the Brothers Parker in 1886.

The fourth daughter, Daisy, was the only member of the family to retain the surname Wood professionally. She made her first appearance at the South London Palace in 1891 and became one of the most popular pantomime principal boys in northern England. She retired in 1928, making her last appearance at the Manchester Hippodrome.

The fifth daughter, Rosie, teamed with her cousin, Alice Archer, known as Lal, to form the Sisters Lena. They made their début at the Varieties, Hammersmith, in 1893, and then went on to appear at halls in London and the provinces, as well as in pantomime in Brighton and the East End. Alice Archer dissolved the partnership in 1896 and continued working as Lily Lena, a popular comedienne in Britain and America. Rosie also turned solo and continued working until her death during the run of 'Cinderella' at the Ilford Hippodrome in 1944.

For a time, the two youngest children, Sidney and Maude, appeared as a double act.

2 Later the Paragon, then the Mile End Empire.

3 The song marked the turning point in Elen's career. Up to then, he had been singing eccentric songs; from then on, he was a coster comedian.

4 It was while Marie was at the Oxford that her portrait was painted by Walter Sickert. It appeared in *The Yellow Book* in April 1894. Later in his career, Sickert told his wife he had destroyed a number of his music-hall canvases because they took up too much room. He had offered one to Katie Lawrence. But she said she would not have it – not even to keep the draught out from under the scullery door! (*A Free House*, ed. Osbert Sitwell, Macmillan, 1947).

5 Lady Somerset had particularly personal views about impurity. She left her husband, Lord Henry Somerset, the Comptroller of the Queen's Household, when he fell in love with a young man. He fled to Florence, a popular resort for expatriate

homosexuals, and occasionally met his brother, Lord Arthur Somerset, who had fled to France after his connections with a homosexual brothel in London's Cleveland Street were revealed.

6 Since her last visit, Koster and Bial had gone into business with the sometime inventor, composer, opera impresario and cigar manufacturer, Oscar Hammerstein I, the grandfather of Hammerstein of Rodgers and Hammerstein. They had also moved uptown to a larger theatre on Thirty-Fourth Street.

7 Since 1894, they had split from Hammerstein in dramatic, if not comical, circumstances. Koster and Bial had become irritated by Hammerstein constantly referring to their music-hall as his. The breaking-point came over a French singer, Mademoiselle de Dio. Koster wanted to book her; Hammerstein did not. Koster, determined to assert himself, booked her for a week. On her first night, Hammerstein took a box next to one occupied by her suitor, a champagne salesman called George Kessler. When she appeared, he hissed her long and loud. Every head in the theatre turned to see who was making such a commotion. When they realised it came from the theatre's owner, they burst out laughing. But it did not end there. In the corridor behind the boxes, Hammerstein and Kessler started arguing with each other. The argument turned into a fist fight, which spilled on to the street. At that point, the two men were arrested by the police. Koster and Bial bailed Kessler out, but left Hammerstein in his cell. After protracted litigation, the two men parted company from their erratic partner.

8 It was while Marie was at the Alhambra that she appears to have made her first film – *Animated Portrait – Miss Marie Lloyd*. Only 50 feet long, it shows her coming out of the theatre, meeting a friend and returning to the theatre with her. Three other films followed – *Marie Lloyd's Little Joke* (1909); *Marie Lloyd At Home and Bunkered* (1913), and *The Man Who Made Good* (1917). There may have been another – *Cinema Revue* (1914) – but no one has seen it.

9 Charlie dated his music-hall career from about 1894 when he sang Gus Elen's song "E Dunno Where 'E Are' at the Canteen, Aldershot, where his mother was appearing. He joined the Eight Lancashire Lads when they appeared in pantomime at the Theatre Royal, Manchester, in the 1898/99 season.

10 The Queen's funeral was conducted by Stewart Headlam's detractor, Frederick Temple, who had become Archbishop of Canterbury in 1896.

11 Between 1903 and 1915, Marie recorded several of her songs: 'Actions (Speak Louder Than Words)'; 'The Coster Girl in Paris'; 'The Coster's Wedding'; 'Every Little Movement Has a Meaning of its Own'; 'A Little of What you Fancy'; 'Now You've Got Your Khaki On'; 'The Piccadilly Trot'; 'Put On Your Slippers'; 'Revue'; 'The Tail of a Skirt'; 'The Twiddly Wink'; 'When I Take my Morning Promenade'; 'When the Leaves Are Falling'; and 'Woman's Opinion of Man'.

12 In Chicago, the police stopped Sophie singing a song called 'Angle Worm Wiggle'. She took the matter to court, but a judge backed the police. In Atlantic City, she was barred from singing 'Who Paid The Rent For Mrs Rip Van Winkle, When Rip Van Winkle Was Away?'.

13 To underline his point, Stuart disclosed that, over a recent six-month period, he had

collected these royalties from his compositions: 'Little Dolly Daydream' – 16s 11d; 'Lily of Laguna' – £2 1s 3d, and the musical comedy 'Florodora' – £33. In fact, no composer suffered more from the pirates than Stuart. They were not outlawed until 1910. But that was too late for Stuart, who was, in any case, wildly extravagant. By 1914, he was bankrupt.

14 Marie's last move was to Woodstock Road, Golders Green – a house she had built to her own design, an ever-changing idea. The builders were given fresh instructions each time she came to see how things were going.

15 Benjamin Keith built up a string of variety theatres in the eastern half of the United States under the United Booking Office. The other half of the country fell under the domination of the Western Vaudeville Association, which ran the Orpheum theatres. Their interests were eventually fused in the Keith-Albee-Orpheum circuit of theatres, which became the Radio Keith Orpheum organization, best known for RKO-Radio films.

16 Marie never liked her husband, whom she dubbed the Half-Crown King (he was always borrowing half-a-crown to buy a drink).

17 Many years later, the home in Hilldrop Crescent became theatrical digs. Many entertainers playing the Finsbury Park Empire stayed at the house in which Belle Elmore had been cut to pieces.

18 Before the controversy about the Command Performance raged, one of Marie's opponents from the past met his end. W.T. Stead, who, through a growing interest in spiritualism, became convinced he was a reincarnated Charles II, was one of more than 1,500 people to lose their lives when the *Titanic* sank.

19 When Ruby Miller appeared with Marie at the Tivoli, she apologized for the language to be heard from Marie's dressing-room. 'I feel it must shock you terribly' she said. 'I just wanted to tell you it isn't me. It's that bloody crowd from Brixton.' (Miller 1933) And when Ada Reeve introduced Marie to Wilfred Cotton, her second husband, Marie's first remark was 'Ain't it bleedin' cold, eh?'. Cotton replied 'Yes, Miss Lloyd, it is indeed chilly.' Marie to Ada: 'Blimey! you've picked yourself a toff all right.' The po-faced Miss Reeve said Marie 'seemed to enjoy making a parade of vulgarity' (Reeve 1954).

20 Another of music-hall's old opponents, Frederick Charrington, was still crusading against alcohol. In a protest about the drinking regulations at the Commons, he burst into the House during a debate on pensions and seized the mace from the Speaker's table. But, before he could make his protest, he was overpowered and placed under arrest.

21 By her own admission, Naomi Jacob (Jacob 1936), Marie's first biographer, is shaky on details, such as dates. She did not get to know Marie until 1910 and can be trusted only after that date – and then not always.

# BIBLIOGRAPHY

Agate, James (1945) *Immoment Toys*, London: Jonathan Cape

Barker, Felix (1957) *The House that Stoll Built*, London: Frederick Muller

Beerbohm, Max (1954) *Around Theatres*, London: Simon and Schuster

Bell, Anne Olivier (Ed.) (1978) *The Diary of Virginia Woolf*, London: Hogarth Press

Bell, Leslie (1961) *Bella of Blackfriars*, London: Odhams

Bennett, Arnold (1932) *The Journals 1896–1910*, London: Viking Press

Bettany, F.G. (1926) *Stewart Headlam*, London: John Murray

Booth, Charles (1902) *Life and Labour of the People of London*, London: Macmillan

Booth, J.B. (1943) *The Days We Knew*, London: Werner Laurie

Bristow, Edward J. (1977) *Vice and Vigilance*, London: Rowman and Littlefield

Busby, Roy (1976) *British Music-Hall*, London: Paul Elek

Byron, George Lord (1886) *The Complete Poetical Works of Lord Byron*, London: Geo. Routledge

Chant, Laura Ormiston (1895) *Why We Attacked the Empire*, London: Marshall and Son

Chaplin, Charles (1964) *My Autobiography*, London: Bodley Head

Charrington, Frederick (1885) *The Battle of the Music-Halls*, London: Dyer Brothers

Churchill, Randolph S. (1966) *Winston S. Churchill Vol 1*, London: Heinemann

Churchill, Winston (1930) *My Early Life*, London: Macmillan

Coborn, Charles (1928) *The Man Who Broke the Bank*, London: Hutchinson

Cochran, Charles B. (1932) *I Had Almost Forgotten*, London: Hutchinson

Desmond, Florence (1953) *Florence Desmond By Herself*, London: Harrap

Dickens, Charles, *Sketches by Boz*, John Macrone

Dickens, Charles, *The Uncommercial Traveller*, Chapman and Hall

Dictionary of National Biography (1903) Oxford University Press

Eliot, T.S. (1951) *Collected Essays*, London: Faber

Farson, Daniel (1972) *Marie Lloyd and Music Hall*, London: Tom Stacey

Findlater, Richard and Powell, Mary (1979) *Little Tich*, London: Elm Tree

Fleetwood, Frances (1953) *Conquest*, London: W.H. Allen

Foster, George (1939) *The Spice of Life*, London: Hurst and Blackett

Frow, Gerald (1985) *Oh Yes It Is*, London: BBC

Gallagher, J.P. (1971) *Fred Karno, Master of Mirth*, London: Robert Hale

Ganzl, Kurt and Lamb, Andrew (1988) *British Musical Theatre*, London: Bodley Head

Gibbon, Sir Gwilym and Bell, Reginald W. (1939) *History of the London County Council 1889–1939*, London: Macmillan

Gilbert, Douglas (1940) *American Vaudeville*, New York: Whittesley House

Glover, Jimmy (1911) *His Book*, London: Methuen

Godfrey, Dan (1924) *Memories and Music*, London: Hutchinson

Goodman, Jonathan (1985) *The Crippen File*, London: Allison and Busby

Gray, George (1930) *Vagaries of a Vagabond*, London: Heath Cranton

Green, Abel and Laurie Jun., Joe (1951) *Show Biz from Vaude to Video*, New York: Henry Holt

Greenwall, Harry J. (1936) *The Strange Life of Willy Clarkson*, London: Long

Henderson, Mary C. (1973) *The City and the Theatre*, Clifton, New Jersey: James T. Whitehead

Hicks, Seymour (1939) *Me and My Missus*, London: Cassell

Honri, Peter (1973) *Working the Halls*, Farnborough, Hampshire: Saxon House

Howard, Diana (1970) *London Theatres and Music-Halls 1850–1950*, London: The Library Association

Jacob, Naomi (1936) *Our Marie*, London: Hutchinson

Laurence, Dan (Ed.) (1965) *George Bernard Shaw. Collected Letters*, London: Max Reinhardt

Laurence, Dan and Rambeau, James (Eds) (1985) *George Bernard Shaw. Agitations: Letters to the Press*, London: Unger

MacQueen-Pope, W. (1947) *Carriages at Eleven*, London: Hutchinson

Mander, Ray and Mitchenson, Joe (1965) *British Music-Hall*, London: Gentry

Mander, Ray and Mitchenson, Joe (1971) *Revue*, London: Peter Davies

Marston, William Moulton and Feller, John Henry (1943) *F.E. Proctor*, New York: Richard R. Smith

Miller, Ruby (1933) *Believe Me or Not*, London: John Long

Mort, Frank (1987) *Dangerous Sexualities*, London: Routledge and Keegan Paul

Mozart, George (1938) *Limelight*, London: Hurst and Blackett

Newton, H. Chance (1928) *Idols of the Halls*, London: Heath Cranton

Randall, Harry (1930) *Old Time Comedian*, London: Sampson Low

Read, Jack (1985) *Empires, Hippodromes and Palaces*, London: Alderman Press

Reeve, Ada (1954) *Take it for a Fact*, London: Heinemann

Roberts, Arthur (1927) *Fifty Years of Spoof*, London: Bodley Head

Robinson, David (1985) *Chaplin His Life and Art*, London: Collins

Rose, Clarkson (1964) *Red Plush and Greasepaint*, London: Museum Press

Ross, Don, Unpublished memoirs

Rust, Brian (1979) *British Music-Hall on Record*, London: General Gramophone Publications

Sandall, Robert (1947) *The History of the Salvation Army*, London: Nelson

Scott, Mrs Clement (Margaret) (1918) *Old Days in Bohemian London*, London: Hutchinson

Senelick, Laurence, Cheshire, David F. and Schneider, Ulrich (1981) *British*

*Music-Hall 1840–1923*, Hamden, Connecticut: Archon Books

Shaw, George Bernard (1932) *Music in London 1890–94*, London: Constable

Sheean, Vincent (1956) *Oscar Hammerstein I*, New York: Simon and Schuster

Sitwell, Osbert (1947) *A Free House*, London: Macmillan

Speaight, George (1975) *Bawdy Songs of the Early Music-Hall*, Newton Abbot: David and Charles

Thorne, Guy (1913) *The Great Acceptance*, London: Hodder and Stoughton

Tucker, Sophie (1948) *Some of These Days*, London: Hammond

Watters, Eugene and Murtagh, Matthew (1975) *Infinite Variety*, Dublin: Gill and Macmillan

Wood, J. Hickory (1905) *Dan Leno*, London: Methuen

Zellers, Parker (1971) *Tony Pastor*, Michigan: Eastern Michigan University Press

The *Era, Entr'acte* and *Encore* were used extensively, as was a series of articles written by Alice Lloyd in *Lloyds Sunday News* in the weeks following Marie's death.

# Index